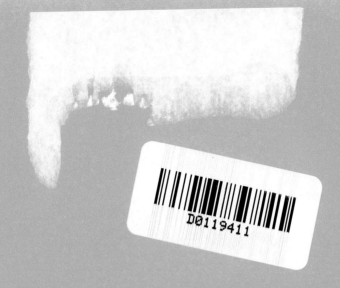

D0119411

The Best Most Awful Job

The Best Most Awful Job

TWENTY WRITERS TALK HONESTLY ABOUT MOTHERHOOD

EDITED BY KATHERINE MAY

Elliott&Thompson

First published 2020 by
Elliott and Thompson Limited
2 John Street
London WC1N 2ES
www.eandtbooks.com

ISBN: 978-1-78396-486-4

Commissioning Editor: Olivia Bays
Publishing Director: Sarah Rigby
Senior Editor: Pippa Crane
Operations Manager: Marianne Thorndahl
Copyeditor: Jill Burrows
Proofreader: Meg Humphries
Typesetter: Marie Doherty
Jacket Designer: Melissa Four
Legal Advisor: Victoria Shore
Publicist: Emma Finnigan
Client Publishing Director, Simon & Schuster: Sarah Anderson

Printed in the UK by TJ International Ltd

CONTENTS

INTRODUCTION

Katherine May

I used to think I had some kind of problem with the word 'mum'.

It started in pregnancy with the phrase 'mum-to-be': the sense of dislocation whenever I heard it. It was so righteous, so compact and smug, so certain. Mum: a fragment of baby talk pasted onto an adult woman, a self-contained palindrome. The brooding hen tapping her bump, a mug of tea (decaf) in hand. I was already sick of her, looming on the cover of every book and pamphlet, the clean, smiling woman, self-satisfied.

Her belly was like a balloon. It had always looked so light before I had one of my own, but now I knew how heavy it was, how laden.

That was before people started calling me mum. Years before my son could even approach the word, other adults borrowed it as if it were their own: *Pop onto the couch, Mum*, they would say. *And how's Mum today?* There were a million facetious answers to a question like that, though I knew better than to give them. I broke, finally, during an appointment for his first vaccinations, when I was too nervous to contain myself. 'I'm not your mother,' I snapped, and instantly felt guilty. But it was painful, this loss of my name at the exact moment that I felt I'd lost everything else.

I knew that I should be vigilant about postnatal depression, but I wasn't expecting it to arrive in the first trimester. It was the otherworldly shock of it, I think: I had been assured that I couldn't conceive. I turned up pregnant at my first IVF appointment, which the nurse told me was not uncommon. This was certainly a wanted baby, but I just didn't expect him to come so soon. I was bleeding, too, for the first eight weeks, and so I was going in for weekly scans: just a pulsing blob at first, which in time morphed into a gummy bear, and then, gradually, into the cartoon-headed baby that I recognised from other people's scans. I had miscarried two embryos bigger than this, and I was grateful that had happened before I'd seen what I now saw on the grainy screen. It was nothing, nothing at all, but also everything. And I knew that I was supposed to carry on and be brave and capable, but I was not brave and capable. I could eat only white foods (my husband once handed me a bowl of cornflakes and I wailed, 'Too floaty! Too yellow!'), and every time I sat down, I woke up an hour later, still upright.

Trying to be brave and capable one day, I travelled into London on the train and ended up locked in the toilets of Tate Britain, sobbing, and being urged to come out by the cleaner. She took me to the cafe and gave me a glass of water. I felt as if I'd been hit by a brick: everything was black and terrifying. It was all I could do to catch the train home again and get into bed, cursing my own weakness, my ingratitude.

This set the tone for my pregnancy, and my first years of motherhood: I was desolate without understanding why. One night, when my son was three months old, I confessed on Twitter that I was depressed, and was struck by the uncanny silence. What I was feeling was unspeakable. Nobody wanted to hear it. One woman direct-messaged me to say that I should get help immediately, because I would no doubt be affecting my child's emotional development. It was coruscating: the immediate assumption was that my love was lacking, not my happiness. Not for the first time in my life, I felt like a different species entirely.

It was another four years before I got an autism diagnosis, but that is a story I've told elsewhere. What I want to say now is that I became a tiny bit more comfortable with that word, 'mum', when I could understand why I was struggling. And I grew to like it a little more when I was editing the essays in this collection. Because in reality, 'mum' has only rarely been the bland, smiling white woman with the helium bump. The true, dirty business of motherhood is a constellation of experiences. That is the only universal: everybody finds their own way through.

When we were commissioning the essays in this collection, we asked contributors to write as though it was a given that their mothering was good enough. Write about the things you'd tell your friends, we said. You don't need to qualify what you say. You don't need to apologise.

That doesn't sound particularly radical until you remember how much of our parenting is hidden behind the front door. We put the certificates and the rapturous holiday photos on Facebook, and keep the dark moments of doubt to ourselves. We hide the conflicts with our partners that Sharmila Chauhan reveals so recognisably, and we tamp down the simmering 'maternal rage' that Saima Mir identifies (a phrase I will now use forever). And it's no wonder we do: after all we live in a culture that actively judges our parenting, from acid comments about the children of celebrities to the tuts and glares that come when a child is too exuberant in a public space. Hollie McNish captures this with great fire in her essay, pointing to the many shocking ways in which life isn't designed with mothers in mind.

Many of our authors find themselves on the edges of that identity, anyway. As an adoptive mother, Michelle Adams shares her fear that she might not be the parent her daughter wants, while Jenny Parrott recounts her life as that most maligned beast, the stepmother. Susana Moreira Marques muses on her reconstituted family, and Emily Morris explores the feeling that, as a single mother, she is not quite enough of a family for her son. Peggy Riley pulls back the hospital sheets to show us the life of a mother who never carried a baby to term, Javaria Akbar grapples with an unplanned pregnancy, and Jodi Bartle explains why she can't stop having babies. The closer you look at motherhood, the more unstable it appears as a category.

These multiple versions of motherhood have always been there, if a little hidden beneath the persistent image of that jolly, inflatable woman. But perhaps contemporary motherhood comes with an extra set of dilemmas and anxieties, conjured into being by our fear of doing it all wrong, and the judgement that may follow. Charlene Allcott considers how to fall in love again when your first love will always be your children, and Dani McClain makes a passionate case for seeing the bigger picture when writing for and about black women who parent alone. MiMi Aye ruminates on the heartbreak of raising children in an age of rising racial tension, and Huma Qureshi wonders whether she should do more to help her sons feel connected to her Pakistani heritage. Meanwhile, Josie George meditates on life as a disabled mother whose own physical constraints can't help but affect her son's freedoms, and Joanne Limburg tells us what she's learned as the autistic mother of a neurotypical teenager. Michelle Tea delves into her internal debates as the queer mother of a son who seems determinedly cis-gendered, and we walk alongside Tiphanie Yanique as she reflects on the meanings of marriage and mortality when children are dependent on you.

If this book is full of questions, then there are also some hints at answers. Carolina Alvarado Molk found her way back to herself through reading about other women's experiences of motherhood, while Leah Hazard makes an impassioned case for knowing our bodies as well as midwives do. But another answer also emerges, loud and clear, from between the lines: we need to talk about all the different ways of being a mother. Even when we don't relate, we can listen. Sometimes there's strength in knowing that there's more than one way to get by. Sometimes we see a version of ourselves in lives that might otherwise feel alien to us. Either way, we learn that complexity is something to be celebrated.

Does this anthology represent the sheer diversity of motherhood? Not even close. That's partly because a fully representative collection of essays would sprawl across your bookshelf like the *Encyclopedia Britannica*; maybe it would never end. There are still many voices we're not hearing – mothers who already find themselves under an uncomfortable level of scrutiny, who don't feel entitled to express dissent, or who haven't yet found their way into the world of the professional writer, with all the amplification that brings. In my own working-class background, women would have found it absurd to theorise the brutal fact of life that was mothering, despite making jokes about its hardships. There was a real terror of exposing the flaws in your parenting – the kids home alone after school because everyone was working; the inevitable dips in mental health – for fear of attracting the attention of social services, or 'bringing the police to our door'. The mothers who write here have a means of expression, and the social permission to express anger, doubt and ambivalence. Not every woman feels quite so safe.

That's not to underestimate the courage of many of the essays in this collection. We invited our writers to choose a part of their personal experience that they felt was rarely seen, freed from any obligation to pretend that everything's perfect. Women know from experience that this invites sneering: these ungrateful, ineffectual, selfish mothers, airing their dirty laundry in public. I think many of us are ready to weather that storm in order to tell some necessary truths. This is a book of brilliant writing, full of images that will stay with you, phrases to be reused, stories that break your heart or make you laugh. Arguments that cut to the quick. Perspectives that you might feel relieved finally to hear out loud. Given that none of it's my own work, I'm unreasonably proud of this anthology. Had I not already had the pleasure of editing it, I would have guzzled it as a reader.

At its core, this is a book about love. Love, in its truest form: complex, frustrated, compromised, argumentative. White-hot one moment; cold as metal the next. I always think this is the most authentic love, and it's what I feel for my own child: fury, rage, adoration. All at once. It's nothing to be proud of. It just *is*.

Whenever I hear women reaching for the moral high ground 'as a mother', I think of all the appalling thoughts I've fostered since I gave birth; of the small children I've secretly damned to hell for hurting my son's feelings; of the acres of landfill I've filled with disposable nappies (and I was in no hurry to potty train); of the distinct urge I feel to protect him above all others. When he was two months old, I was driving home one afternoon and another driver cut across me suddenly at a junction, forcing me into an emergency stop that left the baby seat juddering behind me. In that moment, if I could have caught them, I knew I'd have killed the driver with my bare hands. Something about that experience sums up motherhood for me: it's savage and raw, and not entirely in my control. Good doesn't really come into it.

This is not a book about self-sacrificing, pure-of-heart, bleeding-breast saints, but neither is it a book about how terrible we all are, how degraded, how seethingly desperate for gin. It's about the strange places that love takes us, the peculiar feelings it evokes, and the winding paths we tread. It's a snapshot of reality, told in twenty dazzling voices; the best job in the world, and simultaneously the most awful. Because motherhood is everything at once: pleasure and pain, anger and tenderness, light and shade. In short, true love.

WHAT YOUR MOTHER
DIDN'T TELL YOU

Leah Hazard

'Bilateral paraurethral grazes': three words that make every midwife wince, cross her legs and tut in sympathy. We know exactly what this means; we know the very specific, broken-glass pain it causes; and we know the ways to soothe that pain. 'Pour a jug of warm water over yourself when you pee,' we advise. 'Keep your sanitary pads in the freezer.' We are able to probe gently – so, so gently – with gloved, searching fingers, pushing back petals of flesh to find the damage done – damage your mother never told you about or, at least, not in these terms. She might have said, 'I tore', or 'I was cut'; she might have told you it was 'never the same down there'. She might, in all likelihood, have said nothing.

But we midwives know the parts, and we know the pain, and we name it all. 'Down there' is not just vulva and vagina; it is rugae, it is introitus, it is posterior fornix, it is fourchette. We know the myriad ways in which mothers' bodies stretch and gape to accommodate birth; we know the bits that nip and pop; we have seen the ways they burst, snag, sag and distend. We name the part and how it breaks and, in doing so, we give women power. To name is to identify and to acknowledge. And in acknowledging these womanly wounds, we open the door to healing.

Although I've now seen the female body break and heal in ways I never knew were possible before I became a midwife, my younger self knew of only one route for babies to enter the world: surgery. Both my brother and I were born, for our own particular medical reasons, by elective caesarean section. Growing up, it seemed normal to me that a mother's belly could be opened to reveal the baby curled inside, like the innermost layer of a Russian doll, and then resealed with a long, thin line of spooling suture – the vertical, 'classical' incision popular in the 1970s – ready to be unpicked for any future births. Our family folklore held no tales of hectic hospital dashes or waters breaking onto bathroom floors; I knew only this open-and-shut version of human reproduction which was, to my young mind, neat, clean and normal.

Twenty-five years after my birth, I, too, found out what it felt like to be split open and a child lifted out; my first daughter was born by emergency caesarean section after a long, futile labour. My own wound was a more modern 'Pfannenstiel' incision – a horizontal slice across the lower abdomen, a gruesome smile that has faded over time to a thin, silver seam. The pain was searing and new, a burning throb in the deepest parts of me. The postnatal ward should have been a haven of comfort and love; for me, it was the whirling epicentre of a junkie's fever dream. I wore a morphine pump around my neck and clasped its button in my clammy palm, pressing furiously in the night to release opiate pulses into my bloodstream at regular but still inadequate intervals. Eventually, time played its famous part as the great healer; only now, after years of midwifery, do I realise how lucky I was to have had such a straightforward recovery. I have seen caesarean wounds spraying fountains of serous fluid; I have met women whose wounds can be smelled long before they are seen; and I have seen abdomens puckered with rubbery adhesions years after the original scar has healed. I was sliced and sutured but I was one of the fortunate ones. My child and I had emerged relatively unscathed from our ordeal; we lived and – even more miraculously – we loved each other.

The arrival of my second daughter was, by comparison, faster and virtually harmless. Here, with a vaginal birth at home, I ventured into territory that had remained unknown to my own mother. There was no way she could have told me what that would be like, how it would feel, or how it would change my body or my soul and – not yet being a midwife at the time – I could only guess at the ways my anatomy would rise to this new challenge. As it happened, I laboured for a scant two hours after my waters broke, and my girl shot out with relative (and here I must emphasise relative) ease. Seconds later, I lay back against the pillows of my own bed in a haze of relief, my legs splayed loose and wide while the midwife examined me, her brow knitted with the kind of concentrated scrutiny I now know well; I closed my own eyes and sighed. For all I cared in that moment, she could have driven a freight train through my vagina and I wouldn't have flinched; I was lost in exhausted euphoria.

'There's just a small, first-degree tear on one of your labia,' she said, sitting back. 'It doesn't really need to be sutured, but I can certainly stitch it for cosmetic reasons, if you like,' she added, looking first at my husband, who kneeled by the bedside, and then at me. My husband looked as shocked as I was by the midwife's request for his approval, and he gave what can only be described as the correct answer, which was 'Whatever Leah wants. It has nothing to do with me.'

And indeed, it has nothing to do with him. The tear, as you can imagine, went unstitched. It healed into a small, smooth notch; easily lost among the folds of my anatomy unless you know, as I do, where to look. I carry it with pride; it is both a war wound and a medal of valour, my lasting prize for a moment of glory. This notch – this 'cosmetic' flaw – is not something about which my mother could possibly have told me; nor do most women speak of their own such notches and nicks. I know now, as a midwife, that almost every woman who has had a vaginal birth will bear its marks for a lifetime; millions of us walk this earth with intimate scars and seams, from the tough tissues of poorly healed episiotomies to the almost imperceptible grazes where a baby's hand or shoulder slid by.

Your own mother might not tell you about such things; she might not have the knowledge or the experience to do so; the candour or the desire to share. But the midwives can. We can name the many layers of the perineal body; the labial tears; the deep apexes and the shallow; the edges opposed and unopposed. In naming them, we begin to heal, and in doing so, we impart some of our power to the women in our care. Your mother might not have had the words, or the power, but you can. Know the words, speak them aloud, tell the story. And heal.

ON THE SHOCK OF A SURPRISE PREGNANCY

Javaria Akbar

The first pregnancy test I ever took was in the toilets at a mosque. I was newly married and not ready to have a baby, I told God, as I peed on a stick in the solemn atmosphere. I was relieved it was negative.

Since then I've had two planned-for positives, many negatives and now an unexpected (and medical marvel of a) positive. As the saying goes, the only guaranteed form of contraception is abstinence.

I took that last pregnancy test in the tiny understairs loo at my house, nine years after the first one and as a mother of two who was done with babies, ready to return to full-time work and ripe with delicious day-dreams of writing in an office free from sticky Calpol syringes and baby socks sandwiched between her laptop screen and keyboard. I had just about clawed my way out of the bottom of that lonely well of motherhood, locked my fingers into the ridges of the rocky ledge and felt the sun on my face. My husband and I had put our house up for sale in preparation for moving to a new city and I'd polished up my CV in a bid to give freelancing the old heave-ho.

And then, as the two lines appeared, I felt as if someone had stood on my knuckles with an old, heavy boot, pushing me back into the darkness. The walls were closing in, my insides about to be squeezed out like slime from a toddler's fist. Was this really happening?

This desperate feeling was far removed from how I felt when I took the tests that resulted in my now seven-year-old daughter and two-year-old son. Back then, I was excited, my brain filling up with ideas of nurser-ies and maternity wear, breastfeeding and parenting books. I felt a surge of connection to my husband (which eventually turned to revulsion when morning sickness kicked in and his cologne smelt of dead raccoon). Everything was shiny and new, revelatory and full of cheer.

This time I wanted to swear out loud but my vocal cords were paralysed by shock. It felt as though someone had put my judiciously planned blueprint for the future in the shredder.

This time there were no revelations to look forward to because I knew exactly what being a new mum would entail. And it is this: motherhood is an infinite, relentless slog from which there is no rest or recuperation. Instead of the adventure it is made out to be, parenting small children is a ceaseless labour, often devoid of acknowledgement, recognition and appreciation.

Night feeds are harrowing, haemorrhoids appear, mastitis rears its ugly boob and you never get to switch off or return to the old you. In fact, the old you is dead and you must accept that she will never come back. Your work is unseen and undocumented. You feel left behind, falling further and further away from 'real life' until your career becomes a speck in the distance.

You can't catch up. You don't even know who or what you are trying to catch up with any more.

And yet, despite the exhausting periods of fluster and fatigue, I decided to do it all over again in the hopes of accruing more of those moments every mother is privileged to experience – first words, walks in the park, messy hugs, inexplicable laughter and a constant, living reminder that plans are not concrete canon but flexible formulas that will change from second to second no matter how much you try to steer things your way.

It took many days of remapping my imagined future to get to this point (writing about my experience while five months pregnant and merrily considering baby-boy names). It wasn't an overnight decision. One key step was breaking the news to my mum. She lay resting under the warm duvet in my guest room and sat up like a jack-in-the-box when I told her.

We talked about her own six pregnancies (two unplanned) and she told me that my life would naturally change shape to make room for another, much like her own had. She reminded me that the future I was so fixated on existed only in my mind. I was grieving over something I never had. Talking about all the dinners she cooked, the PE kits she packed and the fevers she nursed me and my siblings through, I realised that I was looking for acknowledgement for my hard work in the wrong place.

Appreciation is not to be found among peers or parents, among preschool teachers or sisters. Nor is it to be reflected in a job title or in the numbers on a pay cheque. It's to be found among our children.

The sacrifices my mother made for me? I acknowledge, value and appreciate them. As an adult who's willingly surrendered to the resolute demands of her children and quashed many wishes of her own, I now understand the deep complexity behind many of my mother's decisions. Her sacrifice was intangible to me as a child until I became the one doing the sacrificing as a grown-up. I am forever in her debt. Indeed, by nature, the priceless labour of motherhood is a phenomenon that perhaps cannot be truly repaid in kind: instead we pass it onto our children, who then become conduits for the love we give them. We pay it forward, baby by baby, person by person.

This coming baby is an unexpected gift, not just for me but for my children, who will gain another friend for life, a co-conspirator who knows them inside out and keeps their secrets. There is much satisfaction in knowing that I have had a hand in creating a trio of people, a little network of chubby buddies.

I think I felt so desperate in that understairs loo because I'd forgotten that motherhood is two opposing things at once: it gives and takes, satisfies and drains, elevates and submerges. It is a long game of peaks, troughs and plateaus – a privilege and a pain. It is a life work that leaves a legacy. If no one reminds us of this, if the smoke and mirrors of patriarchy and self-doubt cloud the truth, we must remind ourselves that our work is invaluable.

My children are the beating heart of my exist-ence, the dogged bass line to the song of my life. They write the permanent melody and I redraft the lyrics over and over again, snapping my pencil a thousand times along the way because no creative endeavour is without its missteps and meanders.

I know this from my own writing – rethinks, reviews and amendments along the arduous route make it far stronger than I originally envisaged.

There is no escaping the uncertainty of life, nor its beautiful, ugly chaos. We must embrace its unexpected twists, dead ends and bridges, its red lights, surprises and blessings. Because, without them, are we really living?

MATERNAL RAGE

Saima Mir

We don't talk about maternal rage. I mean the kind that simmers under the surface of countless women; the kind that makes you dig your nails into your fists in an attempt to stop the fury from entering your hands, because if you don't stop it now, it will turn to something shameful. Mothers dare not speak of it. We are afraid to admit to it, even to ourselves.

Before we enter the world of motherhood, we see only images of pristine kitchens, sleeping babies, the perfect work–life balance. The drudgery that is the reality of motherhood, the long list of unfinished tasks, the never-ending laundry, and the constant silent scream of the mental load, are kept from us. To some extent we play our own part in this, the pull of biology being so strong that we disregard the bits of motherhood we don't want to see before we ourselves get there. But I'm not sure it is possible to understand fully the highs and lows of motherhood without having experienced them.

Pregnancy and motherhood left me raw, unable to process comment and criticism. I was lucky; I had a group of NCT friends who were all experiencing the same emotional rollercoaster. But I would approach the subject of my children tentatively in front of others, worried about judgement, not wanting to bore them, worrying the work of motherhood wasn't exciting. Discussing the reality of motherhood requires real vulnerability.

'Buggies used to be invisible to me, and now I feel invisible,' a new mum confides as I collect my son on the first day of nursery. Her truth makes me inhale sharply. This level of vulnerability is the norm since I became a mother. Maybe it's because time is short between wiping noses, holding snacks, and answering questions about God, the universe, and phonics, but relationships develop faster when you have children. Or maybe it is because we are so desperate to be seen that when someone stops and shows interest, we reveal ourselves instantly, in a barrage of oversharing that is met with nodding heads and knowing eyes.

This invisibility is the foundation on which my maternal rage stands. I'm a mother of three. I love family; not just the idea of it, but the messy reality of unconditional love. Yet at the same time, the reality of motherhood has been viscerally brutal to me.

I met my husband in my mid-thirties. He was ten years older, and we both knew time was short. But children didn't happen for us instantly, and after three years we gave up. And then it happened. And it wouldn't stop happening. In our case, babies were like buses: they all seemed to come along at once.

Six years on, three little boys tear around our house. They are loud, like the battling cowboys from a John Wayne western, their energy levels set permanently to high. They drag each other around the room on a blanket, as the baby crawls between them, narrowly avoiding death. 'Darling, please don't do that,' I say, over and over again, until my head starts to hurt and my own politeness annoys me.

'You wouldn't tolerate this behaviour from anyone else,' says my husband. He's right, I wouldn't. His words echo around my head, mixing with the shouts from the boys and demands for food and toilet trips and toys, until I can't bear it any longer and my volume rises, the sinews in my neck tighten and all I want to do is scream: 'Will you just fucking stop trying to fucking kill each other, motherfuckers!' But I can't say that because I'm the adult. And they are my children and I've seen those ads on TV where kids sit crying in rooms.

I open the fridge and I eat my feelings. I make yet another cup of tea. I vacuum up more crumbs, push my rage further down as I pick up books with newly missing pages. I keep trudging on through the drudgery but the incessant demands keep coming, and then I step barefoot on a rogue piece of Lego and it's game over. I scream.

I scream like a banshee, because it's all I can do. Because I've tried everything to make the fuckers listen. Thinking steps, time out, taking away toys. But children who are loved discover boundaries by pushing their limits. And so I howl like a wild animal, and they turn and look at me with their big brown eyes, all three of them. The six-year-old with his worried face, the baby who's surprised by the strange noise coming from Mama, and the three-year-old who looks hurt and frightened. And all at once I feel I've failed. I am empty and I am awful.

I scoop them up and onto the sofa. In a huddle and under a blanket, we eat ice-cream and watch CBeebies, and I wonder why we couldn't simply do this before. Why was I trying to hold it together with carrot sticks and educational games?

I can see how the path to maternal rage – spewing into abuse – is incremental.

I am lucky. My husband comes home from work just around the time my cup of rage runneth over. He's a good man. He scoops up our children, asks about their days, and takes them upstairs for bathtime as I stand muttering in a corner or shaking my head at the day I've had. He calms the seas with his warmth and his smile. He files away his day until the boys are in bed. I am aware that not everyone has this. I wonder how single mothers cope. But I am also aware that he bears the brunt of, and exacerbates, my maternal rage. My position is so precarious that when he forgets my hatred of sweetcorn and adds it to our pizza, it tips me over the edge.

Because it's the numerous times I have to tell my children to put their shoes on in the morning. It's the swimming/PE/games kit, it's the youngest demanding milk, and the middle child doing his best to be disruptive. It's my husband trying to pacify me when he's just waltzed in from taking too long in the shower and is now heading out the door. It's when I ask for help and he responds by requesting specific instructions on how to navigate the kids out of the house.

'You're tired and lonely,' says another mother when I mention the lack of respect afforded to mothers and the complete disregard for the mental load we drag around all day.

She's right, I am tired. I am tired of the patriarchy. Maternal rage is about more than just the difficulty of raising small children. It's a consequence of all the things that women have to endure throughout our lives. That we are expected to slot ourselves into a work system created for 1950s men; that, despite legislation, women still have to worry about telling employers they are pregnant, still struggle to get by on maternity pay, and then still have to pay extortionate childcare costs in order to go back to work. That, despite nods towards a more equitable arrangement such as shared parental leave, the reality is still that working mothers' careers stall or go backwards while their male partners' prospects might even improve.

And those of us who are stay-at-home mothers have another layer of disrespect heaped on us. Because motherhood is unpaid, and unpaid work is not valued. What is a writer when she's not being paid to write? There are moments when I feel as though all I'm doing is failing.

It's late evening. I'm tired but desperate for time alone. Time where I'm not being pulled and jostled. The children are asleep; the incessant demands are on pause. I'm no longer hypervigilant. Instead, I'm mindlessly scrolling through social media, switching between three apps and BBC News, because at least I'd like to pretend I'm informed.

'How did you get through raising kids?' I ask my friends. 'I drank a lot of wine,' says one. I can't help but wonder what kind of state we are in if the only way we survive motherhood is self-medication. Surely, if a man needed to drink every night to recover from his work-day, the advice would be to find another job. Something is deeply broken here.

I have to find a better way through this, so I join a HITT class. I need to feel stronger. I need an outlet for my maternal rage. 'Is it with other mums? With buggies?' I'm asked by a relative, and I feel instantly diminished. The rage resurfaces. My award-winning career, the publishing deal, the TV option, none of it means anything since I gave birth. Why wasn't I warned that my worth and brain would fall out of my vagina with my babies? For all the demands on me, I am invisible.

HIGH ON OXYTOCIN AND TEA

Jodi Bartle

Lying in my own drying blood, I balance my puffy little baby on my alien, ruined landscape of a body. I lay him on my stomach, so recently vacated but still swollen, my bloodied thighs splayed, my nipples grown huge and dark in sacrificial readiness for the eager razor-mouth of a fresh babe. My vulva is bruised and my vagina cut, my uterus still bleeding from the rough removal of a stubborn placenta, a cannula bent awkwardly under the thin skin of my hand. I am at my best, in my favourite place and favourite state, high on oxytocin and tea.

I love motherhood. I love the animal sounds coming from other rooms as women strain to meet their babies. I love the smells and gushes. I am addicted to the rush of pregnancy tests and late-night visits to the labour ward. I love looking out for the mucus plug in my knickers at 40 weeks, the attention of midnight midwives and the feel of rock-hard boobs. I recall the sleep deprivation as a kind of lucid dream state – walking through the world as if through water: slowly, still bleeding, with a baby in my arms whose skin smells of biscuits and yeast. Downy heads and tiny toenails and milk-sour crusty crevices behind little furry ears are my catnip. I could drown in those babies.

I came to motherhood by way of reluctance; my husband nagged me about having a baby for a while and so I eventually said, 'All right, then.' Not for me the Sheila Heti-style angsting over the pros and cons, the should we or shouldn't we, the fretting over the financial implications and probable career suicide. We just went ahead and had a baby and it was much better than I thought it would be. I had, I suppose, imagined that a mewling infant would be the death of all my highfalutin ways. I wanted to be different from all the women who had come before me, and all of them had babies. I had seen the way women chopped their hair off into manageable bobs when their babies came along, gave up on the gym, made peace with their natural hair colour, stopped reading books, started to wear comfortable clothes and lost heel height. Motherhood looked like a boring club to belong to. But that was fifteen years ago; I had one baby and then another, and now I've got six of them.

I did it again and again, filling up our flat with double, then triple bunks, increasing our capacity for noise, mess and chaos as we went along. It used to be quite the funny joke when we told people I was pregnant again, but then it got a bit tired, and friends became mystified. Some are openly hostile when I talk about having more. I get that; it's really odd to desire this life, and bad for the planet and obviously all my children will end up in therapy because they don't get enough individual attention. My career, such as it was, hasn't got very far and when we come around to your place for a party the children will steal all the Ferrero Rochers and might well break a table leg (true story). Where do they all fit, I hear you ask? They don't, really. We just have to move around a lot to let them get past.

Each time I've had another baby, it's been a boy. That fact leads to its own mythology; I am That Woman With All The Boys. Do I want a girl? Yes. Whatever. Shut up. There have been miscarriages – four in all – and people say to me that perhaps I cannot make girls. That once the sperm meets egg, and the X and Y chromosomes tentatively fuse to become my Eliza, my Goldie, my Violet, then something grows wrong. That my womb, open and welcoming to little boys, suddenly becomes hostile: refusing, rejecting and repelling all those little baby girls who would have grown up and come shopping with me, or perhaps saved the world. I don't think so. Other people say it's my husband's fault. I tend to agree. Whatever. I do penises now.

I also do frequent conjunctivitis, threadworms, the occasional bout of nits, athlete's foot, eczema and verrucas. The pregnancies gave me vermilion tiger stripes all down my stomach, which have faded into soft, silvery scars. I have thinning hair with an irritating fringe of regrowth that circles my forehead like a halo. You could probably chart my post-partum recovery through the reappearance of that halo over the years, like counting the rings on a fallen tree. My cervix often feels as if it is falling out of me, and my bladder leaks, coyly, and sometimes quite ferociously. I can't wear most of my clothes because I am still breastfeeding and need easy access, and I am a little bit fat. My bosoms, however, are magnificent.

Throughout this jagged, flawed trip through motherhood, I have fallen foul of the current thinking towards child-rearing best practices. I'm a fan of the Benign Neglect school of parenting. For me, this means that I love my kids but don't make a lot of fuss about them. It means baby-led weaning because purées are a bore – why mash things up when gums do a perfectly good job? It means letting your baby cry it out because you know that he is tired and it is bedtime and you want him to learn to sleep without your help, even if other people think you are a monster. It means never skinning grapes, because – hello – that's what a gag reflex is for. It means letting them climb up high on things and leaving them to explore, and outsourcing the bedtime story to an older brother who reads for cold hard pocket-money cash. It means that sometimes you leave them sitting on a circus elephant in an Italian seaside town at midnight because you did the headcount

wrong when you left (another true story). It means letting them get dirty and take risks, entrusting them and
empowering them. In the end, it means doing yourself
out of a job.

When people marvel at the size of our family and my
appetite for more, I swiftly reassure them that it only
works because I don't care too much. With six children,
you learn to spread anxiety thinly over everyone until
it ceases to have much impact. Each kid has emerged so
utterly different and so completely himself that I know I
am not entirely to blame. Despite the lack of room and
the fighting for attention and the constant bickering in
the morning over cereal portions and whether someone
mouthed 'dickhead' while my back was turned, I know
that they will all turn out OK in the end. Motherhood
tethers me to these people – they are my people. I knew
them when they were fresh and pink and covered in
vernix and I know them now they have armpit hair and
need money all the time. It is divine and banal, infuri-
ating but the most grounding, deeply satisfying thing:
to be their mother.

BY INSTINCT

Huma Qureshi

When I was a girl, my mother tried to teach me how
to cook Pakistani food. She would summon me into
the kitchen and make me stand over huge steaming silver pots, heaps of dry spices simmering in hot oil with
mounds of garlic and ginger, the onions stinging my
eyes. She never followed recipes but cooked by instinct,
throwing in a little bit of this, a little bit of that. It was
a manner of cooking that confused me: at school my
Home Economics teacher insisted cooking was a science
and that ingredients ought to be measured, precise.

My mother would scoff at this and make me stir the spices furiously with a wooden spoon, cumin and coriander seeping into my skin. I would wait until that magic spot when the oil bubbled up and separated a little from the spices and it was time to add the next ingredient. It was normally at this point that I would complain to my mother about having to do this at all and leave the kitchen with a stomp; hot, bothered, bored. Making Pakistani food seemed to take forever and I suppose I thought I had better things to do. Besides, I preferred pasta to biryani or salaan then.

When you grow up in England with Pakistani parents, you understand that the food of their heritage becomes everything they miss, everything they crave about home. Food is always a feast, a celebration, but it is also a commemoration of the places they left behind, the people they will never see again because of distance, time and death. My mother wanted me to learn how to cook to boost my marriage credentials, I think, but also to serve as a reminder of who I was, where I came from – beyond the West Midlands where I was born. To cook my culture, to taste it, was to understand it; to belong.

My three small children do not have a taste for Pakistani food, partly because they insist on eating a spartan diet of boiled eggs and veggie sausages, but also because I do not cook it enough, even though I know I ought to. Sometimes I am overcome with the urgency of it, introducing them to mildly spiced chickpeas ('Look! Little balls!') or presenting them with a version of palaak paneer before a family event so that they do not look confused and declare it disgusting when it's put on their plate. So that, I suppose, they do not seem out of place.

My children are half English, half Pakistani, though you would not necessarily know it to look at them, with their creamy limbs, which are pink in one light and olive in another, and their masses of golden downy hair. 'You are brown!' my middle son told me. 'I am white!' Although I am not that dissimilar in shade to him, this is at least factually true. When I was pregnant with my firstborn, some nights I would startle in my sleep and shake my husband awake. 'But how will he know where he comes from? What am I supposed to tell him? What if we get it all wrong?' He would take me in his arms and tell me not to panic, that we'd figure it all out.

It is easy for my children to know where their father comes from. He was born into a family of farmers with roots settled deep into their Shropshire soil, undisturbed for three generations now. My Londoner sons roam this land like little lions. Sometimes they sit on their uncle's knee and steer a tractor through it too, shrieking with glee. They can stick their hands into it, stain their knees with it, gather its mud under their fingernails. But it's different with me. My being born in the West Midlands does not explain things to them, like why my mother, their grandmother, is browner than me, or why they must not say hello to her but Assalam-o-alaikum instead.

As a girl, I prayed that I might marry for love and not duty. When I did, it felt like my dreams had come true. It still does. My mother gave me her blessing before we married, but she also gently warned me that other people from the South Asian social circle in which I was brought up might watch for us to slip up. We would need to take care, she told me, make more of an effort to bring up our children properly, with a strong sense of religion and culture, to keep gossip at bay. People would judge, she said, and we would become an example of how not to be, of what not to do.

I did not have any children then. Now that I do, I look at them and, more than anything, I want for them to be free to be who they are, rather than to worry about what other people might think, something that haunted my adolescent years. I want them to have the best of both worlds. I want them not to have to choose to be one thing over the other but to find a way to be both, and this is the promise I whisper to them in their sleep. Some people might read this and ask: How? The truth is, I don't know. But I am learning to trust that it is OK not to have all the answers yet. I know only that the act of raising children is so beautiful and so wild, it is impossible to blueprint its details into a set of tickboxes that fulfil cultural demands.

My Pakistani culture is loud and colourful and chaotic. It is alive. It is a mess, it is fun, it is fabulous. It contains my faith. It is my family, the memory of my father – a lovely man. Its language is sweet, always sounding a little like poetry to me even if my efforts to speak it are not so great. It is a place where in difficult times people flock together, doors flung wide open and arms full of food – their expression of love. There are no stiff upper lips here, no polite offerings of sympathy or condolence cards sent in the post; when you need it most, people will hug you, not merely shake your hand. I want my children to know something of this abundance, this warmth, this sense of humanity.

But it is also a culture that demands much obedience and deference, with little room for one's own needs or desires. Of all things from my inherited culture, I struggle with this the most and I am still learning to tread this path carefully. I see how my husband was raised to make his own decisions, follow his own path without requiring permission, and though I grew up argumentative and so often won my own way, sometimes I still feel like a child put in my place or, worse, a disappointment. Sometimes my behaviour is checked, and I am still told what to do rather than asked if I want to do it.

So here is another promise I have made to my children: that they may be whoever they want to be, love whoever they want to love, do whatever they want to do. That I will trust them to do what feels right even if – especially if – it turns out not to be. That my love will never feel conditional.

Though I never did learn how to cook Pakistani food properly and my success with it remains hit and miss, I have discovered that raising children is not in fact unlike Pakistani cooking. There are no recipes to follow, no foolproof measurements, no quick fixes or guarantees. It takes time and patience, practice. It is slow and much depends on the hand that stirs the spoon. It is a little bit of this, a little bit of that. It is following your instinct, trusting that in the end it will all turn out all right.

A HEARTBEAT

Peggy Riley

I cannot find a heartbeat.

The nurse spoke, working the probe inside me, this vaginal probe like an index finger searching for evidence of what was promised in two blue lines, those hopeful stripes on the pee stick.

I cannot find a heartbeat.

Inside me, on the screen, was a lunar landscape: empty, barren, rocky. The nurse could find no evidence of life in me. And I felt, somehow, that I should have known it would go that way.

The women of my family have fertility issues. There is an eight-year gap between my mother and her sister. My aunt struggled to have one child or any more. My mother tried for fifteen years to have me, due to undiagnosed endometriosis. When she managed it at thirty-four, she was the oldest mother any of my friends had ever seen, but when I began my own pursuit at thirty-five, I was not considered particularly old. In the year 2000, Hollywood starlets over forty seemed to be having sets of babies all the time, though their methods were maybe more to do with their earnings than their well-maintained uteri. Even then, the cost of IVF was in its thousands. I didn't go that route. I knew, with certainty, that failing at it, and bankrupting us trying, would end with my head in an oven. I was already a failing playwright; I couldn't stand the thought of failing something more.

I cannot find a heartbeat.

The probe reached deeper in. The nurse said there was no foetus.

No foetus. No viable foetus.

It was only then I sensed that something was terribly wrong. I heard the word ectopic.

They rushed me into hospital.

I was a wanted, wanted child. My mother's love was a laser beam – it could find me anywhere and burn itself into me. It made me feel special. As a teenager, it made me unable to rebel. As an adult, it made me move across the state and then the country to get away. At twenty-nine, I settled in Britain with a man I did not want to make children with. If I had any chance at fertility, those years were dripping away from me, but this was before commonplace conversations about egg freezing. I was born in a desert and I was sure it had invaded me. If any surgeon cut me open as they had my mother, looking for the problem, I figured nothing would pour out of me but sand.

They rushed me upstairs, unprepared, into a room where three other women were dealing with similar complaints. In the bed to my right, a woman had already lost her fallopian tube. Across from me, an ovary. Diagonally, a woman had lost the lot, as had my mother: she snored like a bear on her back, and who could blame her?

I had arrived at Lewisham Hospital with nothing more than a handbag and some dumb hope. I didn't know why there was no foetus or where it had gone.

I didn't know what else I was to lose.

When my mother had 'the scrape', as she put it, she said she got pregnant – just like that. Whether she tried for more children or not, she wasn't successful, and she had a hysterectomy when I was five. They took everything out: womb and ovaries and tubes. She was scooped out and hollow, lying on a sofa in the desert, where we stayed every summer with her mother. My father was only rarely there, and I sometimes wondered where he was. On my twenty-first birthday, my mother told me he had been unfaithful to her for the bulk of their marriage, but I already knew, because I had so often been his chaperone.

It took me a few years to understand why there were other women wherever he was 'babysitting' me – at the enclosure in Santa Anita racetrack or the local cantina, where he would set me on a bar stool and canoodle in a booth. Maybe my mother's desire for me – the idea of me – was its own laser beam. Maybe it shot my father as it had me, so he had to escape her too. Years after his death, I kept waiting for half-siblings to emerge. I wondered if I'd know them by my father's hair or hands, his teeth or eyes. Maybe part of me is still waiting. Once, he had me play basketball with a Mexican boy I didn't know, and I remember thinking – who is this boy? Who is he to you?

All that long hot summer, whenever I drew near, my mother flinched and told me to stay away. Of course, she was afraid of the stitches, afraid of the wound in her, but I didn't understand it, at the time. The dark desert night clicked with crickets. The air itself was charged. It felt as if, any second, a spark would catch and burn the whole thing down.

Hidden behind the pale-blue curtain of the hospital bed, I cried. I was losing something I hadn't known that I had.

The woman beside me, one tube down and angry,

told me not to cry. If you're in pain, she snarled, ring the bell and ask for something. Ask for something, she said, as if all cures could be dispensed.

One in every 90 pregnancies is ectopic, according to NHS figures. This adds up to 11,000 ectopic pregnancies a year, but that is no comfort when it's you in a room full of damaged women, having your hormones monitored.

The hormone hCG, Human Chorionic Gonadotropin, is produced when a fertilised egg is implanted and peaks somewhere between 8 and 11 weeks. I was at about 10½. hCG sustains pregnancy, and the nurses were checking to see if mine was rising – or falling. Rising – or not falling – would result in surgery.

My mother said her mother never liked her. Maybe all daughters feel the same. She said her mother never approved of my father, a working-class man from a broken home in Albuquerque, New Mexico, who had once threatened to kill his own father if he hit his mother again. There would have been no hitting or threatening or even the raising of a voice in my mother's childhood home, a pretty cottage in Pasadena, next door to her grandmother, an idyll of milk and cookies, bridge parties and stiff Manhattans, the Shakespeare Club and black maids in aprons, passing finger sandwiches. What did it feel like to grow up with such awful privilege? I'm glad I do not know.

My father was a heavy drinker and smoked cigars in his leased Volaré. I breathed in his smoke like air. There were nights when he would come home late, or not at all, and others when he'd lurch down the hallway towards my room or raise his hand to hit my mother. I imagine she never told her mother how things were; it would only have confirmed what she'd suspected. I never told friends how things were either; it would have made me odder to them than I already was.

Ectopic comes from the Greek: *ektopos* meaning 'out of place'.

I was out of place in that room full of women. Some of them had children already and felt done with that part of their lives. The angry woman beside me had a tube to spare; she was half my age.

Nurses kept checking my hormone levels, to see if they were dropping.

If they didn't drop, they would have to go in and find that misplaced foetus, take a tube or ovary and shrink my odds at conceiving further. I feared the tools that had split open my mother.

It was only when my hormone levels dropped that they said I was no longer pregnant. The shrinking hCGs meant that the pregnancy was self-resolving. Because I didn't know what that meant, I asked – where is the foetus? – and they told me I absorbed it. I had absorbed the thing in me.

At 10 weeks, it would have been the size of a strawberry. I had absorbed it, like some horrible Greek god. Cronus consumed his children to stop them from overcoming him. Did I not want to be so overcome?

I had consumed the thing inside me like a monster. I was a monster.

My mother told me, not long after I got married, that she was waiting for a grandchild. It was all she wanted, she said. When they released me, I told her what had happened, as if I thought she could make me feel better about it. I told myself I was lucky: women had lost tubes and ovaries and whole wombs, and I was left intact. I probably even believed it, for a time.

I told my husband I didn't want anyone to know what I had failed to do. I told my bosses I had stomach flu, so they wouldn't know what I'd wanted. Because they didn't know I'd been in hospital, they pushed me to get back to work. I went. I didn't tell friends, because I couldn't bear their sympathy. A single word of kindness would have snapped me in two, back then. I didn't ask for therapy, for the pain at losing the only shot I had at motherhood and the hope I might have another seemed impossible things to speak about. All I'd ever had were those two blue stripes on a pregnancy test, the push of the internal probe and the weight of ancestral wanting. I told myself I'd learn to live with my feelings – or teach myself to forget. It must have been evident how much help I needed, though my Puritan stock prided itself on coping.

I was not coping.

I cried. In public. Often. Once, uncontrollably before an Easter table of tiny, furry chicks in a sad shopping centre in Bromley. I drank to numb my feelings. I tried to stop those words in my head: I cannot find a heartbeat. There is no foetus. You've absorbed it.

The last time I saw my mother before she died – suddenly, of cancer – was in the hospital. At her bedside, I straightened her IV line and said I remembered how it felt. She asked when I'd ever had an IV, and it sounded like an accusation, as though I'd never had an injury. I'd had my tonsils out at twenty-one; I could have told her that, but I didn't. Through the haze of morphine, she seemed to understand. It must have been when you were trying to get pregnant, she said.

I was pregnant, I told her. I was pregnant, as if to assert myself against her illness, against the memory of all she'd wanted and all I couldn't bear. She was dying and her line would stop with me.

After she died, I would wake in the night with my mother pressed against me. I could feel her breathing; I could feel her in my bed. It was only then I sought some therapy, to try to understand the feeling of loss and failure that went back years before, an existential emptiness that left me scooped out and hollow, empty as a bowl. Maybe only motherless could I begin to stake my claim on the woman I could be, away from the laser-beam focus of her love and the memory of all the ways I'd failed.

I cannot find a heartbeat, the nurse said, and for a long time I couldn't either. My hope died with those cells, that missing berry I consumed. At least, I thought it did. But there are lots of ways to mother, even if your body won't let you. Now, I baby an enormous golden retriever, who barks in the night if he needs me, whose cries wake me from my deepest, darkest dreams, two floors above. I know my dog is not my child – no one on social media needs to point it out – but doesn't everyone – don't I – deserve to feel a tiny beat of hope?

THE ABSENCE

Emily Morris

We're on the sunny beach at Sitges, a family holiday on the Continent. Behind me are rows of lofty palm trees and boxy blocks of flats. It's 2013. In front of me, my seven-year-old son splashes in the shallows of the Mediterranean Sea. To my left is a bottle of hot mineral water, a rubbery, shrink-wrapped tortilla and a packet of sandy crisps. To my right is the absence.

The absence loves idyll. That's when it slinks in and sits down next to me, uninvited, like a pervert on a bus. Birthdays are a particular favourite; it arrives in the evenings, when my son is asleep and the balloons are shrunken and I'm alone on the couch, picking at cake.

'Mum, come and swim with me!' Tom shouts. 'Please.'

I can't, because I'm guarding my handbag, my phone, the euros. The precious things; none of them as precious as him. Or, in fact, this moment.

My book is in my hand, crumpled with sun cream and sweat, but I can't read it because I mustn't take my eyes off Tom. He loves the water. He keeps throwing himself into the froth, horizontally, then looking back over his shoulder to check whether I approve. When he goes out too far, I beckon him desperately back, flapping my hand violently, mouthing GET BACK so plainly my jaw aches.

I sit as close to the water as I can without the incoming waves touching me. Yesterday, we were on the beach in Barcelona and the sea was rough. I went in briefly to wash off the gritty sand and to cool off from the August heat. I told Tom to wait at the water's edge and watch my bag, anxious and guilty about leaving him even for a second. A ferocious wave snuck up behind me and threw me onto the sharp sand, filling my mouth and nose with seawater and grazing my shins. Caught inside the turquoise swell, all I could think about was Tom and whether he was safe, about how I should have stayed sweaty and sandy and not left him on his own. The sea kindly spat me out right in front of him. He was crying with shock and saying he was sorry because the waves had engulfed the bag when they took me. I didn't care and I told him so, hugging him tight. My camera was ruined. I had only just bought it from the catalogue and will be paying it off in instalments for fifty-two weeks.

So no swimming for me today, no cooling off in the sea. I'd love to run in there, to hitch Tom onto my back as I learned to do when he was a baby, for the pair of us to cut through the cooling water like a magnificent raft.

That's how single parenthood feels, sometimes: as if we are a formidable team afloat no matter what. That I can do anything with my son by my side, or on my back. That it's OK that his father told me he was infertile then did a runner. We can do this! It's what I write about. It's what I shout about.

But sometimes it is lonely and frightening and incredibly tough. The fact often hits me just before I fall asleep: I might never fall in love again; I might never have another baby. Our family might always be the two of us. When my son grows up and leaves home, my work here will be done. It jolts me awake like one of those half-asleep dreams in which you fall over. Afterwards, the absence lies next to me in bed, spooning me tight, and then I'm awake for the night.

I am angry with myself for being miserable, here, on this beach, on this holiday I have been so excited about and couldn't really afford. I am allowed to feel like this when I am in Manchester and it's pissing it down and the house is damp and crawling with slugs and I've arranged a babysitter but no one wants to go out, but I am not allowed to feel it here.

Deep down, though, despite all I write and shout about, I still can't shake the belief that the only way I can truly give my son a good and happy upbringing, and indeed be completely happy myself, is with the assistance of a male partner. This belief is deeply ingrained; it started with picture books and my religious upbringing and carried on in pop songs and movies that were all about getting the guy. You don't think about your life narrative in your early twenties – at least, I didn't. But subtly, silently even, I suppose I must have assumed I'd follow the pattern, end up part of a family that looked like what I'd been made to believe a family should look like.

Not only that, but as I am sitting on the beach at Sitges, I am suffering from acute depression and anxiety. It will be another eighteen months before I get treatment, and after I do, I'll wonder how I lived in a state of near-constant sadness and panic for so long. I am yet to realise that people will still want to have sex with me and even fall in love with me despite my saggy, caesarean-scarred abdomen. I genuinely believe I am condemned to a lifetime of celibacy and misery because of it.

I don't know how to move around in the world and be me but also Tom's mum. It's impossible for me to be as carefree as my non-parent friends, but when I'm around other parents I feel like a shit, knock-off version of a mum. Since I became pregnant with Tom at the age of twenty-two, I've been blagging it. Other mums-to-be swotted up on the part about giving birth. They attended classes with their partners and learned breathing exercises and made birth plans. I didn't want to know. It was like getting to school on the morning of a test and realising that everyone apart from you, even the rebels, has revised. When it came to giving birth, I knew only that it would hurt like hell, take days, and that I wanted all the drugs. I wasn't disappointed.

In the aftermath of the birth, the health visitor insisted I attend mother-and-baby groups, but they only made me feel more inadequate. There, I got a glimpse of another world, in which women had people carriers, houses and husbands. I was single, sharing my teenage bedroom at my mum's house with my baby, relying on hoisting my huge pram onto irregular buses in order to get around. I couldn't breastfeed but everyone else could and did. At the baby groups, people wanted to talk about nothing but babies and their routines and various books and methods on how to make them sleep. I just shoved mine in his cot and, as long as I knew he was fed and clean, let him grumble himself to sleep. This, I learned, was extremely controversial, just like not being able to breastfeed. At one group, when I explained I didn't have a partner, a woman laughed and asked me whether my child was the result of the immaculate conception. I'd go home and scroll through Myspace, wishing I was with my student friends in Manchester, or that my son's father would acknowledge his baby's existence. It helped to blast out music: Detroit techno and the first Arctic Monkeys album, which my friend had brought me as a hospital gift.

'Turn off that noise!' Mum would say when she came home and caught me. 'He's a baby. He doesn't want to hear that racket.' Word in the circle at the mother-and-baby groups was that playing classical music to your offspring made them more intelligent.

There's another family, just along the beach, but they've got the proper set-up that intimidates me. I think about asking them to watch the valuables, but I overhear them speaking French and I am crap at French. I also don't want to disturb them, because they look like they are having a perfect time. They are wholesome and happy, an observation that makes my solar plexus shrivel. There's a mum and a dad and three kids. The mum has a flat stomach, despite this. Unlike me, they had the foresight to bring a parasol to the beach to shield their children from the sun. My mum had skin cancer recently. I slathered Tom in factor 30 but maybe that's not enough.

If I had a partner, we could do shifts with the reading and the swimming. If I had a partner, we could sit up at night when Tom went to bed sharing a decent bottle of wine and I wouldn't neck cartons of Don Simon sangría by myself. If I had a partner, we could take turns to cook tea and clean the strangers' kitchen afterwards. Actually, if I had a partner, we'd have probably been able to afford to rent an apartment to ourselves, instead of a windowless room in someone else's home. If I had a partner, one of us could have carried a parasol on the train to the beach. If I had a partner, maybe he'd be strong enough to carry Tom back to the apartment from the Metro station when he was weary at the end of the day. If—

'Mum, can we make a sandcastle?'

Tom bounds towards me, slick from the sea.

I panic, drying him and telling him to get dressed to buy myself some time. I can't remember how to make sandcastles. My father always helped with that. I remember packets of paper flags from seaside shops; the Welsh one was always my first choice because it was way more interesting than the others. My mum likes to remind me about the time I threw myself out of my buggy and split my head open on St Anne's promenade because my sister had been given a castle-shaped bucket and mine was a bog-standard one. Another holiday, I asked my parents repeatedly precisely how many grains of sand were on the beach and was frustrated with their inability to answer. These are the kind of memories, pale but indelible, that we should be making now. There is no way Tom's memory of this beach can be of his mother saying no to the sandcastle. I have no idea how I am going to do this, with no buckets or spades or flags, but I have to try.

We move further towards the sea, where the sand is damp and more pliable. I start to scrape clumps of it with my fingers. It gathers under my nails and I know I'll be eating grains of it later. I glance over my shoulder and notice that the French family have a castle. It's more like a complex, actually: a multi-turreted behemoth surrounded by a network of looping moats.

I don't tell Tom about the other sandcastle, and I hope he doesn't notice it. I return to the business of clawing the sand. Tom copies me, huffing with the exertion.

'How long is it going to take?' he asks.

'I don't know. Depends on how big you want your sandcastle to be.'

It doesn't look like a sandcastle at the moment; it's more like a burial mound.

'It doesn't really look like a sandcastle,' Tom says, reading my mind.

The tide is creeping closer and the sun is dipping down towards the horizon. It becomes apparent that our creation will soon be devoured by the sea. This whole exercise begins to feel desperately futile.

The mound is substantial now, but it's a funny shape: high and straight at the front with a back that slopes slowly away from the sea. I try to carve a moat around its edge, improvising with one of my sandals. It bends and doesn't work.

I stand back, my hands on my hips, wondering if there is anything I can do to redeem the castle or myself before the sea comes in. We are racing with nature. But then the mother from the family with the superior sandcastle comes over and offers us the loan of a bucket and spade. I say 'merci' many times, then set to work on the moat with the spade. The sand yields easily and soon there's a deep channel around the weird lump. The next wave fills the channel.

'It looks like a hippo,' Tom says.

'A hippo?'

I shuffle away from it on my knees, to get a better look.

He's right: it does look like a hippo, partially submerged in a swamp.

Quickly, I add nostrils and ears and eyes. Now it is uncanny.

'Hippopotame!'

I look up and one of the French children is standing next to me, beaming and pointing at it. Even I know that must be French for hippo. The father comes over and tells me it is very good. I return the spade and thank them profusely in terrible French. They leave the beach, but we stay. Tom wants one more swim in the sea and I can't stop looking at the failed sandcastle that became an excellent hippo. The light on the beach is beautiful and the hippo glows like copper. I photograph my son standing next to it, his beach towel slung on his tiny shoulder, watching the pink sky. I want to leave before the sea steals the hippo. First, I ask Tom to photograph me kneeling proudly next to it. I check my phone and see that half of the image is obscured by his fingertip. I should have asked the proper family to take a picture of us both with it, I think, but then I remember that my son's clumsy photographs are some of my favourites. This is the way it is.

'Will the sea knock the hippo down?' Tom asks.

'Yes,' I say, 'but we've got the pictures on my phone. And I don't think we'll forget.'

We slope back to the train station, debating churros for tea.

Tom is thirteen now and I am single. I did have a male partner, for a while. It was sweet for as long as it worked. But very few things are permanent, I have learned. And that's fine, because not everything is supposed to be. Meeting one person and staying with them and only them for the rest of your life isn't for everyone. Families don't have to look like we're still taught they should look in order to be happy.

We make it work. I don't own a house or a car or have a husband, but I am happier and more comfortable than I have ever been. My saggy stomach doesn't get in my way any more; I've actually grown to view the stretch marks as beautiful things. Tom has no father and no siblings, but he is also happy. We go to the beach and he leaps into the sea while I read or sleep, then we swap. The time we spend together gets shorter every day, but we're good at making each other laugh. I no longer have to pretend to be interested in Disney or *Doctor Who*. We watch cop shows and comedies and documentaries together. Tom is polite and better spoken than me. I embarrass him, naturally, but that's being a teenager's mum. He's taller than I am and he's teaching himself guitar. He picks it up reflexively and starts playing, usually while I'm making tea in our eternally messy kitchen. He has an eclectic taste in music and knows more about it than me. His repertoire's impressive, even though it's early days, and he loves to play tracks from the Arctic Monkeys' first album. At night, I sink into my marshmallow bed, spread out and rest easy. The absence moved out years ago, and it's never coming back.

LEARNING TO BE A MOTHER

Michelle Adams

'Would you like to see her now?' the nurse asked me with a hopeful smile. For an hour we had been discussing my daughter's medical history, the life she had lived for close to four months without me. Moments later I found myself staring into the huge eyes of a tiny girl, her countenance that of a person much older, her hair as curly as corkscrews. Even to look at her felt like a miracle. Despite my smile, her serious expression didn't change. She was too young to understand the implications of our meeting. Yet I felt certain she was looking at the strange woman with tears on her cheeks, and wondering what made me so special that she had to be woken from a nap.

So, I told her.

'I'm your mama,' I said, and with a shaky finger I tickled her tummy. Right then she giggled and reached for me, and I decided it was a sign. When I left the hospital ward I turned to my husband and whispered, 'Finally, we've found our baby.' We were going to be a family.

By that point I had been waiting several years for somebody to tell me I was going to be a mother. I had long believed that, as a woman who couldn't carry a child in her womb, my role was to adopt a child whose birth mother couldn't care for her. I had never felt aggrieved that I wouldn't experience pregnancy or share my genes, perhaps because I was too young to comprehend the enormity of it when I first found out. So, as we began our home study where we live in Cyprus, I focused on attending all the right meetings and divulging the ins and outs of our personal life to a social worker on whom all our hopes rested. It was very difficult at times, but my faith in the process was unshakeable.

'How long do you think it will take now?' I asked as we signed the last of the paperwork twelve months later.

Our social worker shrugged in a way that suggested she'd been in the same situation before. 'I wish I could tell you,' she said. I had gone into that meeting certain she would tell us about a child that was ready to be adopted, but I realised then that I was wrong. There was no waiting child, and after a year of effort it seemed we had achieved nothing. It felt anticlimactic, as if we had been climbing a mountain only to discover the summit was never there to begin with. It was the first time I felt a thread of doubt weave its way into my thoughts.

It was another two years before anybody called us again. During that time, we tried to get on with life, waiting for the call to come. I watched friends fall pregnant and go on to have their babies, and although I wasn't jealous, I can't deny that my fears didn't intensify each time I saw my dreams playing out elsewhere. It seemed so easy for everybody else. They were in control of their own destiny, and I felt as if we were lingering on a forgotten list in some drawer with no idea if or when we might be able to become parents together. At one point we were called into social services, and I convinced myself it was because there had been progress in our case, but it was just for a review. We watched from the corridor as one couple left the interview room, and once our time was up, we found another couple, just like us, waiting for their turn. That night I told my husband that there were plenty of couples just like us, all waiting for the same baby. 'So what?' he asked. 'That doesn't mean they won't choose us.' Right then, I was less than convinced by his certainty.

It's hard not to question your choices when you feel that way, to wonder whether we were going about things all wrong. Eventually, during a moment of desperation and after a potential private adoption fell through, my husband and I met with a surrogacy agency. I sat in a dated hotel reception that smelled of stale cigarette smoke, listening to the representative tell us how easy it would be to have a child, and began to wonder if we should take the easier road. But ultimately, despite the tantalising promise of a short nine-month wait, I knew it wasn't for me. I didn't want any child. I wanted my child, and it was my strong belief that she was coming to us via adoption. In fact, after that meeting, I felt even more certain.

A few months later we got another call, the conversation that would lead us to our daughter, and all the difficulties it took to get us to that point faded to nothingness. When I held Lelia on that first day in the hospital, I knew she was the child I had been waiting for. I'm not a very religious person, but I almost believed that the wait was some kind of test, because to me she was truly perfect, and I felt truly blessed. The first time she fell asleep in my arms and I laid her in her cot, it was as if a line had been drawn between the past and the future. But I was met by a new fear on that day. What if I didn't turn out to be the mother she needed?

An uncomfortable dichotomy emerges from the process of adoption: for my dreams to be fulfilled, first somebody else's had to be shattered. What my little girl had to withstand in the first four months of her life must surely be one of the hardest trials any person has to endure. When Lelia was born she was unable to feed properly due to a cleft palate, and soon became unwell. While we will never know her exact reasoning, we know that Lelia's birth mother felt unable to cope, and after a short time decided to leave her in the care of hospital staff. After that, Lelia spent the next four months of her life in the intensive-care facility of our local hospital.

To be given away by the person on whom you are entirely dependent is a great loss, and I imagine her biological mother too must have suffered an unimaginable burden when making the decision to withdraw from her daughter. And yet there was I, stepping into the role, never happier in my life. That evening, I put her to bed and I had no choice but to leave her in somebody else's care until the next morning. That felt so wrong. I was her mother now, and yet remained at the mercy of everybody else's decisions. Everything I did during that first week while Lelia remained in hospital was scrutinised and evaluated. I knew that, although we were there every day and already felt like her parents, somebody with authority could still have changed their mind. And at that point, had her birth mother decided to return, we would have had no choice but to pretend that Lelia had never been part of our lives. The thought of it was unimaginable.

Because of her cleft palate we had to learn how to pass a feeding tube through her nose and into her stomach before we could bring her home. Seven days later we were overjoyed when we were finally able to leave the hospital, but our homecoming was overshadowed when she pulled the feeding tube out that same afternoon. Passing the tube that night to feed her, I realised the fantasy I'd had about parenthood was over. I stood in my bedroom after she slept and cried. Some of those tears were relief that she was fed, that I'd managed to pass the tube. Some were simply gratitude that she was home, and we could get on with the fact of being a family. But most of those tears stemmed from fear. I had everything I had ever wanted and yet I felt utterly overwhelmed. Perhaps I was better able to understand the fears of her biological mother in that moment than I will ever be able to again.

Although the feeding tube was a necessity, we also knew we had to wean her off it. She needed to learn to use a bottle if possible. We bought every special feeding device we could find and celebrated when, on the one hundredth attempt, she managed to drink 10 millilitres. I became her biggest cheerleader, telling anybody who'd listen about her progress. But even though in hindsight we were doing well, after the tube came out permanently she lost half a kilo, and I felt the weight of the judgement of the medical professionals. When she cried in public and I couldn't soothe her, I felt the disparaging looks from strangers.

I was vocal about our adoption, proud of our daughter and the way she came to us, but despite my positivity I found it hard to bite my lip when people asked me what had happened to her 'real' mother. On most occasions I was gracious, but sometimes I was caught off guard. Simple comments such as 'I never even noticed you were pregnant' felt loaded, as people tried to glean the full extent of our story. Because although I was open with our truth, there were situations where I just didn't have the strength to talk about it all, like being in the supermarket with a crying baby after next to no sleep. Yet when I wasn't open with people or when I got upset by their interest, it felt like a failure on my part. It made me feel as if I was trying to hide something, despite it being perfectly reasonable not to want to discuss my gynaecological history with a relative stranger just because they'd asked. That shame of not talking came down to one simple fear: if other people didn't see me as her mother, maybe Lelia would feel the same way when she grew up.

In the eight-month period before the adoption was finalised, I found myself trying to meet other people's standards, desperate to prove that I was good enough, and that choosing me had been the right decision. Perhaps every new mother feels something similar. I felt anxious when the professionals questioned decisions I had made. I wondered whether it was selfish of me to question the paediatrician, or wrong to seek second opinions regarding her healthcare.

After the court ruling where we were miraculously, and tearfully, declared her legal parents, nothing changed in practice. Not for another couple of weeks at least, when the surgery to repair Lelia's palate was finally undertaken. On that day I carried her into theatre, barely holding it together as they anaesthetised her, telling her that I'd be there when she woke up. For two hours I sat with my husband in near silence as we waited for news. When they came to tell us that she was back on the ward, I ran down the corridor, rushing to her bed. I found my little girl screaming, disorientated, her arms in splints because that was the local practice. Blood seeped from her mouth. I scooped her up, just like on the first day, and held her close. I whispered that Mama was there, and that everything was OK. And this time, despite her pain and my fear, she settled straight away. She reached out, held onto me, and she was soothed. For months I'd been wondering whether I had the right to call myself her mother, but all along the only person who had the answer was my daughter. Since that day, I've never questioned who I am to her again.

CAN I TOUCH MYSELF, THOUGH?

Hollie McNish

'If we can build a successful city for children,
we will have a successful city for everyone.'

Enrique Peñalosa

Six weeks after birth, the nurse looked between my legs
and said I was healing. Then she said, 'You're OK to
have sex again.'

You're OK to have sex again.

And I thought:

Fuck you.

This first check-up after I gave birth to my daughter summed up one of the main feelings I had as a new parent; that, after the initial fuss and present-giving and visits and people telling you how lovely the baby is, no one really gives a fuck about you. For mums, I would add 'or your body', which is now never described as glowing. No matter how bullshit that sounded when I was pregnant, I felt a sudden lack of any positive image for my body after it did one of the most amazing – and gruesome – things it ever will. I'm sure that if anybody went through the process of giving birth, whether vaginal or caesarean, for any reason *other than* to have a baby, then the aftercare would be treated with much more funded seriousness.

I remember my mum telling me not to stand up when I got home from the hospital. For weeks: 'Don't stand too much', and 'Don't carry anything', and 'Put the baby down because you currently have an overly stretched hole between your legs that needs to close properly without internal organs pushing on it so that shit doesn't start falling out of it in years to come.' There is no way a new mother in our culture, especially after a second child, can lie down for two weeks after birth.

Obviously, some people *did* give a fuck about me. I had a huge amount of support. From family and the NHS first of all, to the ninety-year-old women volunteering to serve tea and biscuits three times a week in a small church hall, to the breastfeeding helpline assistants and 3 a.m. internet-forum responders. There were a lot of people who really cared within the bubble of parenting.

But when I stepped out of these private, domestic spaces into the 'real world' (the world I had previously lived in), I felt reality, or society, fuck my shit up. Like when I tried to get on a bus or train, or go anywhere with a pushchair, or go back to work or drive to my parents' house three hours away and stop for a piss at the motorway service station at night. I did a lot of things in early motherhood that I'd never done before and that were not related to being a parent but rather to being a parent in a society where most public spaces are designed for able-bodied car-driving business people with no caring responsibilities.

I pissed, on several occasions, in the dark, squatting behind my car door in motorway service stations because I could not risk waking my child up to go to the faraway toilets. I pissed in the car into a nappy while driving for the same reason. I sat on the floor in the vestibule of more trains than I can count, not because there were no seats or because I did not have a ticket for a reserved seat, but because there were no seats for parents with pushchairs. I remember one of several four-hour train journeys to visit family, sitting on the floor with my daughter, apologising to everyone constantly as they stepped over me and manoeuvred around the pram to get off the train. Sorry, so sorry.

In the UK you can book a seat in a 'quiet coach' so as not to be disturbed by people on phones or hen-dos, but you can't book a 'pram seat' or whatever we could easily call it. Every time I get the train when I'm on tour, I see a carer sitting on the floor next to a pushchair staring into space, feeling, I assume, like a piece of unwelcome shit on a shoe.

As parenting continued, so did my constant apologising. I apologised for my baby crying in public spaces; for feeding my baby in public spaces; for my pram taking up any space anywhere; for my baby gurgling on buses; for leaving my house with a baby and not just staying in a play park pushing a child back and forth while singing 'Old MacDonald' until my brain rotted into oblivion.

Last week I went to one of my favourite cafes for an afternoon of writing. I found it ten years ago by searching 'cafes good for children'. It has a Wendy house and a toy box but also a varied menu for adults, which is abnormal for most baked-bean and squashed-pea child-friendly venues.

I was working on my computer all afternoon in this cafe and at 3 p.m. an influx of parents and small children came in from the primary school next door. After five minutes, I had been apologised to by two mums, whose kids were chatting.

Shush, Billy, look, that lady is trying to work.

After ten minutes another mum apologised for interrupting my peace and shouted at her toddler for rattling a pram. I started counting. After an hour, I had been apologised to over twenty times – mostly mums, but one dad – for children's noises and movements, as I sat working at a table in a cafe with a Wendy house in it. I smiled as much as I could and said things like, 'No problem, it's your cafe too', and 'This isn't my office!' because I wanted to be the stranger who changed their day.

Strangers took on amazing importance when my daughter was little. They are always important, of course, but as a new parent, they were like a daily drug. I found myself in two states of emotion with most strangers. Some, I wanted to grab by the hair and pull across the floor screaming, 'Fuck you, you fucking bastard', including the woman who criticised my daughter's chocolate snack at the end of a six-hour train journey; the man who asked if I wasn't a bit young to have a child; and the five hundred passengers who pushed past me as I carried my baby, luggage and baby bag up the Tube stairs, crying.

Then there were the other strangers, at whose feet I wanted to bow, crying, 'Thank you my kind, kind superhuman.' I found public space such a bitch for new parents that the tiniest acts of kindness – or just, well, not being an arsehole – left me overwhelmed with gratitude. A local cafe with one small box of toys in the corner became an all-inclusive resort; the waitress who asked me if I wanted a glass of water while I was feeding my daughter in a cafe was my new god; the airport play area with about two toys in it made me sob. I developed an unhealthy level of lust for every person who ever held the bottom of the pushchair as I carried it up the stairs.

Motherhood and parenting are often treated like some private domestic issue. But so many of the things that make them so difficult and, in many cases, disgusting and degrading, stem from practical, political, cultural and urban design issues.

I didn't piss in a car park because I was a new mum. I pissed in a car park because of service-station design. I didn't sit in toilets alone breastfeeding because I like to smell other people's shit. I breastfed in toilets because I was feeding in a culture that is so sexually confused that I was made to feel awkward having a baby sucking milk out of my tit, and I was petrified of offending anyone. My friends do not have prolapses because they are mothers. They have prolapses – at least in part – due to underfunded physio, and a culture where checking internally as we squeeze our pelvic-floor muscles, to see if we are in fact just clenching our butt cheeks, is deemed too intrusive. (In France, I am told, every new mother gets pelvic retraining.) The pressures against taking shared parental leave or baby-change facilities in men's toilets show how these issues affect fathers too.

Even initiatives ostensibly designed to be helpful often made me feel worse. BREASTFEEDING FRIENDLY stickers are perhaps the starkest example of this. Were these the only places I was allowed in? For me, these signs left me more confused, as if saying, here is OK but don't even fucking attempt it anywhere without one of these stickers. I'm still in two minds about these.

When I speak to old schoolfriends who are now having their first kids, I'm told that this stuff is getting better. Slowly. Thing is, a few months ago we all met up in a park in London and it started to rain. I had an eight-year-old with me. They had three babies and a toddler between them. We couldn't find anywhere to go and sit and so we huddled in the corner of the underground station for an hour, dreaming that one of the empty office spaces would let us go and sit on their lovely floor with a takeaway cup of coffee. This would be a dream, we thought. An empty office floor.

Back to the check-up.

The nurse looked between my legs at a vagina and vulva that I had been scared to look at since the birth.

I was not upset because the nurse told me that sex – by which she meant penetrative sex with a penis – would now be OK. Maybe there are new mothers who want to know this, who are desperate for sex again or who are wanting to try for another baby straight away.

I was upset because, after looking closely at the most intimate area of my body after one of the most amazing and traumatic things it has been through, this is *all* she told me it was now able to do.

I wasn't told whether it was OK to massage that area again. Or take a hot bath. Or to cycle. Or to do anything else that could be deemed pleasurable. I wasn't told if it was OK to be touched in that area, by a loving hand, whether mine or another's. Could I be licked there? Lord knows we can't discuss such personal things in this culture! Yet we can make it quite clear that my fanny was now able to have someone else's penis in it again. It wasn't even healed fully, but it was healed enough for this.

I am often told I am vulgar or 'unladylike' because I talk about (women's) blood and sex and use swear words. Aside from the highs and the beauty of early family life and the love I obviously have for my child (which of course I need to guiltily state here), for me early motherhood also involved stretching and ripping and leaking and bleeding and vomiting and milking and crying and snotting and then pissing in nappies and sitting on train floors and, perhaps in a few years, an avoidable prolapse. I am so fucking tired of being polite about it all.

BRIEF EXCHANGES

Susana Moreira Marques

Translated by Julia Sanches

I.

It begins with her saying *I've never told anyone* and ends with me saying *neither have I*. And in between, a single sentence on how the love we feel for a child is not necessarily immediate, on how we need time to get to know and fall in love with another being, even though they were once inside us. This takes place over the phone, and might never have happened face to face, looking each other in the eye.

2.

One day, on a noisy street corner, after a casual run-in, she says, raising her voice over the roar of the bus passing us: *but you have a happy family now.*

This *but* presumes: you separated from your first daughter's father *but* you have a happy family now. *But* you found another man. *But* you had another daughter. *But* you rebuilt your life. It also presumes: *but* you know better now. It presumes: you were unhappy once, with your first family, *but* you are happy now. Also: *but* I, with my family, which is intact and not cobbled together or strange, am not happy.

At the look of shock on my face from her pronouncement on my life, she hesitates: *at least, from the outside, you look like you have a happy family.*

This conversation reminds me of Tolstoy, of the opening of *Anna Karenina*. Except Tolstoy failed to add that all happy families are alike 'from the outside'.

We go our separate ways, she probably thinking I might not be as happy as I seemed; and me thinking I might be happier than I'd thought.

3.

In a single conversation, a woman, seeing me with a baby in my arms and sensing how tired I am, says *don't worry, it'll be over soon* and, right after, *enjoy it while it lasts, it'll be over soon*, as though these two statements were not at odds.

4.

At a cafe, a couple with their newborn meets up with some friends who want to see the baby. Presumably, the friends do not have children. It must be one of the first times the couple has taken the baby out; they are keyed in to the slightest movement in the pram. When the baby cries, the mother picks it up right away but does not bring the baby to her breast, as if still embarrassed to nurse in public. They use all of the short space of time in which the baby sleeps to discuss the birth. Rather, he discusses the birth. He tells them everything, the finer points. He describes in graphic detail how the baby had come out of his partner, how she had dilated, opened up, how first it was the head and then the rest of the body. He describes the look of the umbilical cord, its colour and texture, the feel of cutting it. *It was amazing*, he says, and she, silent, nods and averts her eyes.

5.

Two friends, new mothers, discuss the time after birth. One of them makes a confession and the other follows suit; the first woman responds, and the confessions pile up until they are sharing details about the sex they do or do not have with their husbands, and the state of their vaginas. They do this at a table in a public space, without glancing around them, because this public space has become safer than the private.

6.

When my turn comes to be seen at a state agency, a clerk, without asking whether I would like any advice, uses her working hours to instruct me on when and for how long I should hold my baby. She shares in detail her theory on people's habit of walking with babies in arms, and on the benefits of prams versus other means of transportation that would force a baby to be held at their mother's chest, absorbing her scent. In the short time I waited – I had priority, after all – she noted that I had stood rather than sat, had moved around instead of staying still, that I'd muttered and not been silent, and had, she admonished, effectively been rocking the baby. Her sentence is swift: *she will turn you into a slave*. At first, I'm taken aback by the unwarranted intimacy, by her intrusion into my life, but soon it dawns on me that she must have also been a slave, and that she might have deluded herself into thinking there was some way around it.

7.

End of day. Me – exhausted, frantic in the evening chaos, phone pinned between cheek and shoulder, hands busy changing the nappy of the baby who will not stop moving – telling my friend, who's unsure whether she should have a second kid: *but it's so good!*

8.

Outraged no one had warned her of all the things that were not as they seemed nor as people claimed they were, a mother decides to tip off other women. Whenever she meets a woman who is pregnant, instead of saying everything will be fine, like everyone else does, and that she will know what to do when the baby comes – she'll learn from instinct – she speaks of what will go wrong: of how the woman might not have a natural birth, and almost certainly not a 'beautiful' one, about how it can be really hard to breastfeed, and she might not get the baby to sleep through the night, not after several months or a year, or even two or three years, despite all the people who talk about babies that sleep without waking.

She soon realises that the pregnant women don't want to hear any of that. They look at her askance. They change the subject. They say yes, they understand, but it's clear they think it'll be different for them. Nowadays, whenever she meets someone who is pregnant, she simply wishes them good luck and shares contact details for a specialist in maternal and newborn care.

9.

She says she listened to a long radio programme in which a researcher was interviewed about what motivated humanity. The researcher had come to the conclusion that it was not money that motivated humans, nor social status or even love, even though these things might eventually be connected to the thing that motivates us: pleasure. Money facilitates pleasure, as does social status, and we nearly always get some pleasure from love.

Hearing this, the woman had felt as though the researcher's theory explained another enigma discussed at the time: maternal ambivalence. Take her daughter, a new mother. And she, therefore, a new grandmother. Her daughter would leave her house, drop her son off at nursery, and dash to work – an hour-long drive – to earn a salary that didn't allow her to live near her place of work. She'd work seven or eight hours, then dash back home – another hour-long drive – often not arriving in time to collect her son from nursery. His grandmother would pick him up and take him home and, if need be, bathe and feed him. When her daughter arrived, exhausted, with no patience for her son's tantrums, she did so with the air of someone who wanted to head right back out, to escape. But then the boy would say a word he'd never said before, or pull a face that was meant to be funny, or lean into his mother's body as though she were a buoy at sea, and in that moment – even if it was just one moment – her daughter would experience real pleasure.

The conclusion reached by the researcher – that we are capable of extraordinary feats, of unthinkable sac-rifices, of madness and risk-taking for the sake of five minutes of pleasure – could be applied to motherhood. Having been a young mother, and now a young grand-mother, she believed that nothing compared with the pleasure of love for a child, nor with the work needed to win that love.

She debated this at length, more with herself than with anyone else. The concept of pleasure – not to be confused with joy or satisfaction, though it could encompass both, but not necessarily – deserved some consideration; after all it was a complex concept, and for some reason she couldn't figure out, had been given a bad name since the time when she was young, and a mother.

10.

You've planted a tree, written a book, made a child, I am told by people who do not have children and do not know that a child is never made.

11.

The couple realises that the best answer to the question of whether she is their first – knowing the next question will always be whether they'll have another – is: *no, she's not our first but she is our last*. They always laugh, and maybe they realise they can't ask that sort of question the way a person asks if you want to go back to *x* restaurant or to a dream destination you once visited.

12.

As a second-time mother, first-time mothers address me with something like reverence. I soon have the feeling they're disappointed to learn I don't have a ready answer for their questions or any answer at all. Other times, it's as though my failings – my admission that I have no answers or my inability to say whether certain strategies are better than others – are a consolation, making conversations with me paradoxically useful, though I may not have anything relevant to say.

13.

Since the birth of her son, my friend, who lives in another city, regularly sends me messages and photos on WhatsApp. Through these brief exchanges, I accompany her as though she and the baby lived around the corner from me. She sends photos of him sleeping, of him awake and staring at her, of the baby lying in bed while she, lying beside him, watches him, enthralled. On WhatsApp, she shares his first times: for example, a video of the baby's first laugh. Through her, I relive the experience of having a newborn child. I relive it as if it were something new, as if I'd already forgotten what it was like, even though my own daughter was born just a year before my friend's.

14.

Since I recently became a mother, my friend, who does not have children, makes an effort to talk to me about babies. Meanwhile, I make an effort to talk about things that are relevant to grown-ups and to people who do not have small children. It's a well-meaning misunderstanding. It goes on for a while, for longer than a single visit. Until I realise it isn't a misunderstanding at all: I don't want to talk about babies but want people to talk to me as if I still have important things to say about the world; she is tired of the world, of debating interesting issues, and feels comfortable surrounded by the chaos of children in a family home, talking about babies.

15.

I know the story. I've heard it dozens of times, either from mothers or children. Parents separate. Father leaves to live abroad. Mother cares for the child. Father visits from time to time. He rings on Christmases and birthdays. Sometimes he says he'll come but doesn't. Mother manages child's expectations. Child grows up. Father grows old. Father comes home. Father grows close to child. Father wants to spend time with his grandchildren. Child takes their father in and, if he is ill or in trouble, helps him. And yet I've never heard this story told the way it is told by this mother, who is now almost sixty years old and has been a single mother nearly all her life, without a hint of resentment, anger, or regret.

16.

Years later, in day-to-day exchanges at nursery, I am still referred to as 'the mum'. Years later, this continues to shock me and I still fail to recognise myself in this umbrella term. Even though, at home, with my daughters, I constantly talk about myself in the third person, and refer to myself as 'Mum'.

17.

The woman is old. She's had work done to her lips, the wrinkles around her eyes, and her nose, but all this does is highlight her lost youth. Her gaze is unchanged. It is sweet and a little feverish, and is most apparent now, when she's stopped talking and seems to have forgotten she's sitting at a table having dinner with a large group, and looks over at her grown-up daughter, who laughs and chats animatedly, even though she isn't saying anything special, and does not return her mother's gaze.

18.

Before couples become parents, they are told that when they have children, their lives will end. Or, that their lives are just beginning. No one mentions the far more likely prospect that, more often than not, life will carry on just as it was.

19.

A mother will spend the rest of her life wondering if her experiences are the same as those of other mothers. Take, for example, the bewilderment of this mother – who doesn't believe you can predict a child's personality based on their childhood, and who has witnessed how much her daughters have changed – on hearing another mother of more or less the same age mention how her children are unchanged. Her discomfort doesn't stem from the revelation of this discrepancy but from the fear that it isn't so much a difference of experience as it is a matter of knowing who our children really are, and, in this case, that either the other mother is wrong or she is.

20.

Whenever I have to go away for a while and spend time apart from my daughters, for whatever reason, I can't help but notice other people's children. Which is why I find myself saying hello to little kids, striking up conversations with people I don't know, asking questions I do not like to be asked, and showing photos of my daughters to strangers in cafes.

ON STIGMA AND STOICISM

Dani McClain

Not long ago, I was on a live radio show with two other black mothers. The three of us find ourselves writing about black motherhood and family at a moment when the topic is in vogue in the US. Major media outlets are running big stories about the maternal health crisis that looms over our pregnancies and births, about our children's experiences at school, and how our encounters at home and in our neighbourhoods influence what we do at the ballot box. The three of us on that national, midday radio programme had such a platform because of a new interest in broadcasting and publishing perspectives on black family life from those who are actually part of black families. For the time being, expert status isn't reserved for those who scrutinise black families from the outside.

Two of us were not married, and when the topic of single motherhood came up, I spoke to it. Sixty-five per cent of black children in the US live with an unmarried parent, compared with 24 per cent of white children, and these households represent a third of US children overall.[1] In the few minutes I had, I repeated arguments I'd made in my book, *We Live for the We: The Political Power of Black Motherhood*. I talked about how inaccurate it is to label me a 'single mother' given the circle of family and community that's consistently and meaningfully involved in my child's upbringing. I talked about how strange it is that, in public discourse on both the right and the left, the presence of a marriage often erases any question around parental competence, financial stability and children's well-being. Meanwhile, a woman heading a household is assumed to be impoverished and unable to instil discipline and dignity in her children, especially if that woman is black. I talked about how, throughout hundreds of years of enslavement, those near the top of the system's hierarchy routinely broke up black families for the sake of profit or punishment, separating mothers from children, husbands from wives. I talked about the resilience that black people have shown across generations by creating and maintaining strong kinship networks despite disruptions to family such as mass migration in response to racial terror in the twentieth century, and mass incarceration today.

I repeat these points whenever I can, because they're a necessary corrective to entrenched public narratives about the broken, dysfunctional black family. But there is another side to this story, one that isn't getting much airtime: many of us *are* struggling under the pressure of being the sole provider. Many of us *can't* depend on extended family to help, and 'single parent' is an apt description. Many of us are trying to shield our children from the pain of an inconsistent ex's broken promises. And many of us, myself included, run through the range of possible emotions in any given week: exhausted and despairing one day, proud of our life choices and buoyed by love and support the next.

The messages I've received and the conversations I've had since my book was published have helped me to reflect on the need for more nuanced takes on families in which one adult is tasked with the day-to-day responsibilities of parenting. I want more stories about what it's like to handle the dinner–bath–bed sprint solo night after night, juggling meal prep and toddler tantrums or homework meltdowns. I want more accounts of how it feels to bear the weight of a childcare crisis alone, and I want to hear the righteous resentment that comes with knowing that the non-custodial parent gets to go to work regardless of whether there's a safe, reliable place for their child to spend the day. Stories about the trials and tribulations of single parenthood certainly exist, but black women aren't often the ones telling them. I read dozens of books about motherhood in preparation for writing my own and found that black women are largely optimistic or silent on the topic of navigating parenting on our own. One book that bucks the trend is asha bandele's 2009 memoir *Something Like Beautiful*, and its most vulnerable passages are lodged in my mind because during my research I was so hungry for acknowledgement that we, too, are human and suffer when we're expected to be more than that. bandele writes:

> I told myself if I cried I was setting a bad example for my daughter. Others told me the very same thing. Told me never to be a victim, Black women are not victims and we are not weak . . . In the post-welfare-reform days of the alpha mom, I was clear that being a victim, showing any weakness, was punishable by complete isolation and total loss of respect. I was a mother, a single mother, a single Black mother. I was part of a tradition of women who do not bend and who do not break.

Too many of us are blinking back tears of exhaustion or loneliness in the name of saving face and upholding the race. Advice of the sort bandele received keeps us from taking our disappointments and losses seriously enough to grieve them properly. It also keeps our children from fully knowing us and understanding their upbringing. Still, it's clear why we hold tight to our stoicism: if we allow ourselves an honest response to the hardships of parenting alone, aren't we tacitly supporting the narratives that call our families broken, our children doomed? Two-thirds of Americans believe that more single women having children is bad for society.[2] It's hard to believe that a group that already judges us so harshly can be trusted with our families' complex truths.

I'll continue to share the points I made on the radio that day. I'll continue citing the CDC study that shows that black men are generally more likely than men of other races to read to, feed, bathe, and play with their young children on a regular basis, whether or not they live in the same home as the child.[3] For as long as people want to hear what I have to say about black mothering, I'll defend our right to challenge cultural norms and contextualise how and why we do it.

But I also plan to take off the rose-coloured glasses and do more to validate the various experiences of mothers who parent alone. Regardless of how we present ourselves, marriage fundamentalists will do their best to frame us as overwhelmed, inept mothers and pitiable, discarded exes. So why keep shoehorning our lives into position papers and op-eds meant to convince them otherwise? Black unpartnered mothers could instead be writing to and for each other. We could instead be taking up space on the page and on the airwaves with the full expression of our rich and messy lives.

1   'Children in single-parent families by race in the United States', Annie E. Casey Foundation Kids Count Data Center, https://datacenter.kidscount.org/data/tables/107-children-in-single-parent-families-by-race#detailed/1/any/false/871,870,573,869,36,868,867,133,38,35/10,11,9,12,1,185,13/432,431.

2   'The Changing Profile of Unmarried Parents', Pew Research Center, https://www.pewsocialtrends.org/2018/04/25/the-changing-profile-of-unmarried-parents/.

3   'Fathers' Involvement with Their Children: United States, 2006–2010', National Health Statistics Report, https://www.cdc.gov/nchs/data/nhsr/nhsr071.pdf.

ON WORKING OUT WHAT IT ALL MEANS

Josie George

You stand by my bed in your school uniform with a bad case of the Mondays. You have drama lesson today and you hate drama. The early red spots on your nose are almost as angry as you are.

I love you.

You are eleven years old and my only son, but it's me who feels young and small. I am sitting on the edge of the bed looking up at you, my legs still remembering how to stand. You lean towards me, stiff and cross, and

I wrap around you; I push my nose up against your neck and kiss you like a child kisses, like you used to kiss me, rubbing my lips against your skin, and I hear the quiet sound in the air that your wide smile makes as your bad mood cracks like an eggshell.

I want a turn to be made again. I want to climb inside you, to rest in your warm belly, to be free to go with you everywhere – even to drama – but then that moment breaks too and I know I must take charge instead.

'Go on, you. Go and brush your teeth.'

I might not have much freedom or power, but I get to choose what things mean and I like that.

One evening, when the last light had drained away, dripping and pooling underground to solidify into something that could be rolled out again tomorrow morning; after that, when no light was left, we pulled on extra layers and took torches out onto the dark, dirty street we live on because I wanted to make a slow day count for something. You walked beside the mobility scooter I must use to get my body anywhere and your torchbeam jumped and pounced and searched in an echo of your easy chatter. The moon shone dimly, like a shawl had been thrown over it in a hurry so as not to outshine your eager, tiny light.

'Maybe I can make it brighter?' you suggested, stopping to focus the narrow beam upwards.

I smiled at that, my bundled star, my eyes not on the moon at all.

When someone at school asks you, 'What's wrong with your mum?' I think you flounder. I don't blame you.

'Her nervous system doesn't work properly,' you say in the end, defiant, because I haven't taught you a better answer. I feel guilty about that, but 'nerves' is a less confusing answer than 'lifelong chronic fatigue and idiopathic autonomic dysfunction' and, besides, you'd never remember that.

Maybe we should stick with 'M.E.', even though that doesn't quite explain things either. At least people usually shut up with an acronym. Maybe we should throw all the useless words at the wall – all the words that make us small and left out – and tell everyone to mind their own business, but I have taught you to be kind, so we are kind.

On the days I struggle to walk at all, you run to fetch the two walking sticks from the umbrella stand so I can get to the kitchen, the bathroom. 'Let me help you, Mummy,' you say and duck under my armpit to try and hold me up. You seem to quite enjoy it. You're tall enough to push my wheelchair on your own now, on the rare occasions we go into town. You won't let anyone else take a turn.

'I'm not grumpy or cross, I'm just in a lot of pain today,' I'll explain sometimes, so you don't take the things my face does personally.

'You need a hug,' you reply.

We have always gravitated towards my bed like seagulls coming to roost: circling, restless, joyful, inevitable. Partly because this is where I often need to be but also because it is the best and warmest place in the house.

When you were younger, when my head had turned to hot iron, pulling me with some new gravity towards the ground, I would suggest we watched nature programmes on the old tablet, side by side under the duvet. At four or five years old, you'd watch solemnly, pulling at my hands to stroke the soft fur of you as you lay next to me, pink and vulnerable, watching migratory flights, ocean swirl, devouring pounce. I wanted to show you everything.

If I'm honest, I imagined I would wake in you the heart of a zoologist – or an explorer, maybe, or a wildlife photographer. You'd trace a lifelong passion back to these still moments, me breathing slowly, happier beside you. You'd describe the door that was unlocked with the opening of a grey whale's wide mouth and I would have won; I'd have given you everything I have lost. But now, a few short years later, you'd rather watch YouTube and you want to work in an office, which only goes to show how little control we get to wield over others' meaning-making. I suspect it's better and safer that way. How about I decide what this all means to me and you can decide for you.

You often used to fall asleep here, next to me. When you woke, you'd sit up immediately, eyes still closed, then blink them open once: here. Off to on in an instant; you'd cry with the disorientation of it. I'd hold you till we both separately remembered ourselves.

Weekends, I'm more stuck than usual, done in from another week of trying to keep our life bailed out. I float on the opportunity to rest while you play computer games downstairs or watch films or play Lego, using your loo breaks as a chance to steer back to my side again.

'Do you need anything, poppet?' I ask.

'Nope!' you reply, cheerful, and five minutes later I'll hear your bright laughter from the room below and know you are telling the truth.

I have to be careful not to look at my phone on those days. Grinning families on day trips, children clutching sticks in shady woods, holding water pistols, pedalling bikes. It hurts too much. It makes me feel as if the two of us are not a real family. It makes me forget that the same lessons of love and loss are waiting in all these different lives even if *their* bodies work; that all *those* people are stumbling over their own meanings too. I end up resenting everyone and everything.

I have a picture you drew for me in a frame on my bedroom wall: a submarine with three portholes and a smiling face in each. Me, you, the cat. I look at that instead.

'Are you lonely?' I dare to ask sometimes.

'Why would I be lonely?' you reply, baffled. 'You're right here!'

One weekend, it was different. We went to the seaside with my parents and my brother. I sat on the causeway in my wheelchair and watched you throw yourself onto the cold, grey beach. Training the zoom of my camera on your distant body, I watched you take the time to wave your plastic fishing net around the sky, drawing a territory in this new, big air. I watched you christen your unused wellies in the tide and write your name on the dark, wet sand. Occasionally your arm would shoot up in an unselfconscious victory shout. I took a photo of that. It felt like a leaving behind of something, somehow. You explored like a young man, claiming something new to you with your long limbs and your long stride.

From my watching place, I cried a while, the tears bubbling out of me like surf, but it wasn't long before I raised the lens back to my eye and got back on with the business of enduring, got on with laughing and softening and hardening all at once like something old and wild, like something of the sea itself. I am getting good at that.

I remember that I dried my tears and called out for a seaweed wig and for treasure to be laid around me, and you and my brother came and reverently laid two shells on top of my clean, laced shoes. You all busied then, delighted, inspired: my sympathetic limbs. You searched and quested and I played my role as steadfast, smiling deity; safe harbour. I watched you pace back and forth and I was with you; wet sand on borrowed hands, the sink of your boot, my boot. A jubilant shout brought a mermaid's purse the size of my palm; a crab's dismembered claw; the pink angel wings of an open Artemis shell; a closed mussel the shifting colour of night. You found them all.

The red of your coat shone in reflection as you ran along the beach. I gathered the brightness of you into me and kept you safe, along with all the gifts at my feet.

That was another day that I knew again, for a new time, for the thousandth time, what it means to be your mother.

BOYS WILL BE WHATEVER

Michelle Tea

The ultrasound technician, waving her wand across my stomach – a hugely pregnant thing, gooey with conductive jelly – pointed to the screen on the wall and gestured to the tiny nub of penis between my baby's legs. 'It's a boy!'

Me and my wife-who-is-more-of-a-husband (WWIMOAH) looked at each other with wide eyes and goofy smiles. Many times we had spoken about how little we cared what gender our baby would be; boy, girl, what's the diff? What even are such things in today's queer theorylandia? My WWIMOAH is a 'girl' who has opted to lop off their breasts for pleasure, comfort and fashion; a giant skull and bones is inked where their tits once sat, suffering beneath layers of cotton and elastic. Their current hairstyle is anti-racist skinhead meets seventies UK punk meets androgynous runway model. If this is a 'girl', then we must agree on how little information that word provides.

Right then, with our son little more than an amorphous sack inside my body, 'boy' meant nothing more than 'in possession of a penis'.

But, still. As a queer lady, I haven't spent very much time among people in possession of penises. Like many, I've had a father or two, and (like many) they've been disappointments, men who force you to take leave of them at some point, if they haven't already taken it on themselves to bail. Yes, I dated boys in high school, but their gothy hairdos were bigger than mine and we shared lipstick and eyeliner. And yes, I had some male friends, even some best friends, but they were faggots, and everyone knows that the very best faggots are practically girls, or at the very least as repulsed and mystified by men as the average lesbian. And yes, I date trans men, but their paths through the world often have much in common with my own; I've only occasionally felt the alienating values that I routinely experienced in the presence of cis-gendered men. Truthfully, males have always made me uneasy. And now I would be raising one.

'He's a boy – for now' was one way to answer the inevitable gender questions friends and strangers alike ask a pregnant person. And once he was outside my body, a living, breathing little creature, the gender slapped on him seemed both more and less absurd. When strangers on the train, watching him gurgling happily in his stroller, asked me what he 'was', it struck me as the least interesting, most beside-the-point question you could come up with. Who cared? But, at the same time, the energy my son gave off – his vibes, what I felt, in those intensely intimate, non-verbal months, to be his essence – was totally boy. As much as I insisted that it didn't matter, I also knew that it did. I just didn't understand how. Two years into it, now that the moms in our moms' club have dubbed him the 'alpha male' and our relatives have given him the nickname 'Fratty', I still don't know what any of it means.

As much as I loved my son's instinctive love of
sports – his fascination, even as an infant, with watching people playing tennis or basketball at the park; the
way the football games perpetually broadcast at our local
pizzeria held him in thrall; the way he threw a ball like
a thirty-year-old man who made his living doing so
– I also felt a little anxiety, an urge to 'balance' him
by making sure he liked 'girl' things, too. Out shopping, I pushed tutus on him, tiers of colourful tulle
shot through with sequins or stars. 'Do you want this?'
I asked him brightly. His hand shot out: 'No.' Digging
through a costume box at a library, I begged him to
don fairy wings, sparkly headbands, velvety capes. 'No.'
When he did profess to enjoying something 'girly', like
the unicorn sweatshirt I found for him at Goodwill,
or Fancy Nancy books, or carrying his great-great-
grandmother's leopard purse (stuffed with racecars),
I felt an embarrassing amount of joy. I know of many
feminists raising girls who do the same in reverse;
fearing their daughters' love of princess culture may
be toxic, they search for the antidote in train sets and
sports. But in my obsessions about my son's gender I
have come to realise that my 'radical' efforts only wind

up enforcing the outmoded gender assumptions that make me crazy and harm our culture.

It is worth noting that my WWIMOAH shares none of my problems. They are only psyched that our son shows such proficiency in sports at so young an age. They can't wait to coach one of his teams, or for him to get old enough for them to play video games together. My WWIMOAH fits my binary-busted notions of the type of activities a 'female' should enjoy for maximum cultural revolution. Never mind that my own hobbies include shopping for shoes that disfigure my feet, mani-pedis, flipping through fashion magazines – you know, 'girl' things.

By affirming that, yes indeed, baseball and Matchbox cars are 'boy' things and unicorns and purses (and mani-pedis and stilettos) are 'girl' things, I'm actively working against the culture I want to live in: one where activities and animate objects are not gendered or employed to police the gendered expectations we have of our tiny humans. Realising this, I felt dizzy with overwhelm – the gender problem of our culture is so big, so pervasive and insidious, was there any way to think outside it? But once I regained my equilibrium, I felt something else. Relief.

Acting as though the dismantling or upholding of the patriarchy rests on the shoulders of my two-year-old son is madness. Feeling a responsibility to actively 'queer' my son is similarly stressful. At the heart of these impulses is a simple desire for my son to grow into a good man in a world too full of bad ones. With few models for good men beyond the queer community, it makes sense that I turned towards tutus and fairy wings, but like every other parent, it's my duty to honour who my child is in this world, and hold the largest possible vision in my mind for how his unique personality will manifest as he grows.

In 2016 a photo made the internet rounds. It showed a bunch of high-school athletes – boys, really – wearing T-shirts that said 'WILD FEMINIST'. It appeared in the wake of Trump's gross minimalisation of sexual assault as 'locker-room talk', after which men who spend lots of time in locker rooms began speaking out about how unacceptable and abnormal such conversations are. Sure, it was intended to sell a product, but the boys appeared to be genuinely down with the message. My heart skipped when I saw it. It feels embarrassing to be so gratified by this image, to need so deeply a model of young cis-gender maleness that is blatantly feminist. But considering how popular that photo was, I'm sure I'm not alone. The old white men holding culture back will all be dead soon enough; will the next generation of males have a better, humbler understanding of the world and their place in it? I could see my son among those guys, a little dude among dudes, totally chill with calling out misogyny because, duh, patriarchy is bullshit and feminism rules. While some boys will be girls, more will be boys, and this is how I want them – horsing around in their locker rooms, wild, feminist.

THE PSYCHIC

Charlene Allcott

I've never been a runner, literally or figuratively. When facing fight or flight, I roll up my sleeves and take off my earrings, unless there's a third option available – do nothing at all. I will wait in the rain for buses; remain in jobs with no prospects; endure a relationship when it's way beyond saving – until the day I didn't.

And when that happened – the moment I called time on my marriage – I was shocked by the strength of my urge to run. All I wanted was space between what I was becoming and who I had been, and a friend with a car willing to make that happen. Natalie had always been my ride or die and luckily this time I only needed a ride. I said, 'Get me far away, to another country if possible.' She drove to Wales.

All break-ups are a variation on a theme, whether three dates in or after vows before God: when it ends you doubt who you are and wonder who you were, and you look for another pair of arms to fix that. My girl took me to a festival, a place with the promise of open arms. We sat in the sun and drank 'fuck it' champagne; danced till the early hours and pinned flowers in our hair; but the men – the men who could give me answers in the form of validation – they seemed alien. I wanted to offer a whole lotta woman, but all of me was mum. So, drunk and confused, I did something desperate: I went to see a psychic.

The fortune-teller had a tent on the edge of a field and boasted qualifications from a top psychic academy. Mike didn't look like a mystic; he looked like a mortgage broker or a chemistry teacher, and he said, 'You're here because of a relationship.' Which is like a dentist saying you're there for your teeth, but because I'm bad at quitting I stuck the reading out. I let Mike consult his runes and, after conferring with the spirits, he looked me straight in the eye and said, 'You're scared.'

'No shit, Mike,' I said. 'I'm scared of everything. I'm scared of being alone; I'm scared of starting again; I'm scared of the recycling with its never-ending list of rules.'

But he removed his specs and shook his head and said again, 'You're scared. You're scared of all those things but there's something else.' And because he was a stranger and because of the 'fuck it' champagne and because I couldn't be sure he wasn't in fact psychic, I was honest.

'I'm scared that no one will want me.'

Without pause Mike said, 'Well, that's bullshit.' And we laughed, Mike and I and any spectres in his tent. As I stepped back into the sunlight, I estimated it would take a year to prove him wrong.

The first kiss was easy. Kisses, you get for free. I took myself to the club and pretended to belong; under the low lights I could be childless and incautious. And I didn't have to tell the man anything, I simply stared at his beautiful face until my intentions became clear and aside from steering his hands away from my flanks, it was fine, like riding a bike – sweaty and wobbly and freewheeling. He didn't care that I was a mum because the bass was too banging for him to hear that, but he couldn't ask me back to his because his girlfriend was there waiting for him. I didn't mind. I had someone at home too.

I knew I had to be where the seekers are: the apps and the sites, the late-night clubs of the world wide web. 'No single mums.' They put that, brazenly, at the bottom of otherwise humdrum profiles. Like back in the day when they put 'no blacks' on ads for damp bedsits, or today when they say 'no benefits'. Those apps needed a reduced aisle, a shelf at the back near the blackcurrant squash, where I could sit with the damaged and the out of time. And I did feel damaged.

They dragged my son out of me like he was a stubborn weed and put me back together with a blanket stitch. At my six-week check I told the doc I'd been too scared to look, that if it looked how it felt I'd see yesterday's corned-beef hash. She said, 'It's fine. You'd never know.' And she meant, 'He will never know, this man you're thinking of', and I was relieved because that's how women are supposed to be, immaculate and untouched. I don't blame the men. I blame myself and the product aisles and the magazines and all the other ways we troll ourselves. I blame all that for making me feel I had to hide.

I rebuilt my profile with no evidence of my sinister child-rearing ways and it didn't take long for someone to walk into my web of lies. He took me to the river, he bought the drinks, he told me I was sexy and I was drunk enough to believe it. We played twenty questions; with the right enquiries you might guess who I am. The wine made me loose and I let my status slip. He coughed into his glass and said, 'I didn't know you had a child.' He said, 'I hope I don't offend but I don't want to date a mother.' He didn't offend. I know the rules of romance: rejection is part of the deal and, although I believed him, I decided he would break this rule for me. I – someone who buys microwave chips – imagined that with enough effort I could change his mind; I'd show him my stretch marks and he'd abandon those once firm values. It nearly worked.

I manic-pixie-dream-girled myself into his affections. I stayed up late and drank shots and didn't once mention school catchment areas. When he asked what

I wanted, I said adventure when the truth was some sleep; I projected a spontaneous existence while my days were ruled by nap times. For our first night together I booked a hotel, the perfect backdrop for anonymity. But eventually motherhood ended our dalliance because he said he wanted me waxed, and parenting doesn't allow time for that. After him, I said I'd no longer conform: I'd grow out my body hair, give up bathing, find the man who loved me for me and not an illusion. If the spirits were right and someone was to want me, they had to want all of me. All of us.

He came in the form of a friend, so stealthily I almost didn't notice. He offered something mothers don't always receive – help. Rather than flowers he bought blue-top milk; instead of chocolates, armfuls of bog roll. I offered myself as both a woman and a parent, and he told me the combination made me special. Single motherhood had become my superpower, snot and snacks my shields. I no longer had to pretend and it was such sweet relief to relax my vigilance. It wasn't long before he asked me to stop running, requested that we stand still together, and I let him into our life.

When you date as a single parent it's like doing everything at once – the spark and thrill of early days alongside the gentle intimacy of domesticity. I adored it all. I was greedy and bloated with love. The first time I watched him read to my boy, adapting his tone for each character, I died. When I was resurrected, he was cooking dinner. I thought I had cracked the code. I was unprepared for our first and last fight, the wind on the seafront so fierce he had to shout: 'Good luck finding someone to play daddy!' Parenthood is not a game; if it is, it was one I was losing, along with hope, along with him.

All break-ups are a variation on a theme. I lay awake wondering who I was and doubting who I'd been but motherhood doesn't give a shit about heartbreak. With another dawn, my son needed cuddles and comfort and Weetabix. We were two once more and I had my answer. Mike the psychic was right. I will always be wanted.

AN HONOUR I PROBABLY DON'T DESERVE

Jenny Parrott

My stepchildren were only three and four when I met them, thankfully after their parents had divorced. I was woefully ignorant of all things to do with bringing them up. But their fierce little faces when their dad introduced them to me set their cards out on the table. They weren't to be won over by my suggestion that we feed the ducks in the park. When we got into the car and the radio was playing softly, Louis, the three-year-old, declared he hated loud music (he forgot this as a teen), while later Josie announced that I was mean for turning the television off and, by the way, *Mulan* was the very best film.

I had been an only child and after my father's death when I was nine, it had been just me and my mum. I had relatives but they lived a long way away, and so my teenage and adult years were pretty much child-free. I can't ever remember holding a baby or taking a toddler's hand. Now these children were looking at me with a deep suspicion. And I was terrified, as well as incredibly wary of them.

Not quite terrified enough, though, to avoid setting up home with their dad. But the sort of scared that means you get everything wrong *all the time*. I didn't do anything the way their mum did, so a black mark there; I didn't know that Louis didn't eat anything green (clearly another black mark); and obviously I couldn't read them a story in the proper way. I managed to upset everyone – their mum and dad, and the parents of all of their friends – by trying too hard at a birthday party for Josie at our house, spending weeks collecting trinkets for pass-the-parcel (socks, fun lip glosses, sparkly bracelets, even an electric toothbrush), all hidden in layer after layer of cheery wrapping paper. The scathing looks from all concerned stayed with me for a long time. How could I not understand that pass-the-parcel was layers of *newspaper*, with a single *sweet* hidden in each layer? Apparently that particular East Dulwich rule wasn't in my DNA. But how can you know these things if this is the first children's party you've been to, let alone helped organise?

I didn't learn. When Josie declared she wanted to bake a cake for her mum while her dad was out, I allowed her to choose a Nigella Lawson recipe that cost £42 for the ingredients alone. It was my first attempt at a cake, and very possibly Josie's too. It was inedible.

Louis was simpler to deal with. He detested me. Whenever his dad wasn't looking, Louis would do a silent impression of the Incredible Hulk, teeth bared in my direction and fists clenched as he trembled with rage. He was adept at pasting his meek choirboy expression back on in the nanosecond it took for his father to turn around. Until Louis was eight – so nearly five years after we met – I never dared challenge him. Then one lunchtime I cracked, and Louis and I yelled at each other from opposite sides of the kitchen table, with me shouting, 'You *will* help me clear the table', and him yelling, 'I won't!' I can't remember who won – Louis, almost definitely – but we got on much better after that.

As the years passed, slowly the tide turned, and a few teenage moments aside – the sneaked weekend party in the house when their dad and I were away (now notorious in our family history), an argument when Louis and I screamed at each other in the street (which I'm sure the neighbours enjoyed), the shenanigans with alcohol during 'band practice' in the loft during Year 7 – we all became good friends, probably because I was more lenient than their mum and a softer touch for cash than their dad. We started to listen to each other, and to enjoy each other's company. I discovered to my surprise that I really like teenagers (even in large groups) and their continual dramas, and I was happy to sit for hours gossiping with whoever was around.

It was during this period that I learned that being a stepmum can be a very privileged position. I think children of divorced parents want to be the best version of themselves for each parent, and this means that to some extent they filter what their birth parents are allowed to know. While I'm sure that I wasn't told everything, there were times when I heard things in confidence, and I made sure never to breathe a word. I knew there might be a time in the future when I could properly be of use for a much more serious problem, but I wouldn't be approached if I'd already proved that I couldn't be trusted.

And I learned too that perhaps being a stepmother is *easier* than one might anticipate. Leave the adult stuff to their real parents, and you learn that kids want to be with people who like them, while stepmums and stepdads want to like their stepkids, not least because it makes life easier. It's not perfect as a scenario, of course: few would dispute that the full set of one's original, loving parents (whether mum and dad, mum and mum, dad and dad – whatever) is ideal. But the world isn't perfect, and for many the blended families of today are supportive and caring alternatives that work surprisingly well. Looking back, I can see that families are curiously resilient, and I'm just sorry it took me years of hindsight to realise that. I could have enjoyed it all much more at the time if I'd allowed myself to. Nobody but me much cared if I got it right or wrong.

Today my stepkids are adults, and what lovely grown-ups they have turned out to be – lively, funny, chatty, kind and compassionate. Josie and I talk nearly every day (indeed we were texting each other at midnight last night, making each other laugh), and while I don't speak to Louis as often, it feels, on my side at least, that we have a deep bond that can't now be broken. Every Christmas he gets me the very best present of all the gifts I receive – I don't know how he does it, but each year he gives me exactly what I need, even if I didn't realise that I did.

I used to say that I couldn't take any credit for how these kids turned out – they have two parents who put in all the hard graft to guide them securely into adulthood. But the truth is more complicated than that: Josie and Louis changed me, and I think in some small ways I influenced them. What I feel now is very proud that my stepkids and I have *chosen* to love and support each other. I think of them as the gift that continues to give to me.

Being a stepparent is tricky, and inevitably it arouses a complex set of emotions. The children themselves aside, you are essentially flung right into the midst of the relationship of their actual parents, which really isn't a very comfortable place to be. But when at junior school my stepdaughter was being bullied, and she described to me what had been going on, I was suddenly overwhelmed both with love for her and a Vesuvius-like desire to protect her. And in that instant I knew that I would lay down my life for either of my stepkids without a moment's hesitation, and be happy to do so. I don't think that will ever change, and it feels an honour that I probably don't deserve.

THE DISHES

Sharmila Chauhan

Our daughter cries every time I orgasm. Her wails cut through my own sounds, slicing through our already compressed pleasure. When she was a small babe, I would put her on the breast and nuzzle her back to sleep. But she's three now. I grab some clothing (if indeed I had time to undress), rush her back to her room and ease her between the covers. At this point, I have been known to drift off holding her hand. But if all goes well, I return and we attempt to resume. Sometimes the task can seem insurmountable; my daughter can interrupt a second or even a third time, and so what began as a beautifully connecting moment becomes a mechanical invitation to get it done, and get it done fast.

It wouldn't be so bad if we were just looking for something to take the edge off our continued sexual curtailment, but there is more to this than that. A relationship is like a mirror that cracks when children arrive. It's what you do with the pieces that counts.

For us, life has become a carefully constructed mosaic of moments. But these interrupted attempts at intimacy are beginning to create gaps, and pieces fall off the mosaic and onto the floor, cutting our feet as we make our way, half sleeping, to the bathroom or down to the kitchen to make a 5 a.m. breakfast. They hang around my neck, reminding me of things undone or lost.

Morning: I rush to get myself and the children ready, the acid guilt licking the edges of my stomach. I haven't done enough. I wish I hadn't been too tired for sex last night. It was late and I was exhausted. My body yearns for a connection deeper than the domestic, but today I have to undertake a double school run, food shopping, house admin, phone calls, school pick-ups, dinner, and prep for my class, before heading out to teach in the evening. I can manage, of course I can.

I make tea and ignore the dishes stacked high from last night. My husband sits in his dressing-gown, eating breakfast; says something about assuming that I'm not going to do the washing-up. He alludes to an agreement, pre-children, where one of us cooks and the other cleans. Of course, we didn't factor in sleepless nights, washing children, dressing children, feeding children, checking schoolbags, packing after-school snacks – etc., etc. – into this model. Suddenly I am angrily running the tap and emptying the dishwasher. Anger bubbles hard through my blood. My heart tightens. Tears begin to fall onto the immaculately clean plates.

When I was a young girl, I stood in the snow while my father showed me how to change spark plugs. We were out for so long that I lost feeling in my feet, but my dad's look of pride warmed me right to my bones. He taught me that there was nothing I couldn't do if I set my mind to it: I was entirely equal to men.

By the time I met my husband, I had just finished my PhD and was writing a novel. We were two stars in the sky, twinkling individually but stitched into the greater scheme of things by our shared views and desires, and our admiration for each other. We were intense and romantic: endless conversations, late-night love-making, art, friends, family all merging into a thickly woven blanket that kept us warm. We travelled well together, planning to marry in Thailand. After that, we would take a year off to do what we loved most: more travelling, reading, writing and being together.

But then I fell pregnant. Unplanned but not unwanted; our first child was conceived during our wedding recce in Koh Pha Ngan. Back home in London, a thin blue line pierced through all I had planned for our future, and suddenly I was very afraid. To my mind, we were both financially and emotionally ill-equipped for this baby. My dream of beach wedding, travel and a novel were being sucked into my womb by the little creature that nestled nonchalantly between my hips.

Pregnancy brought some of the usual physical changes: nausea, exhaustion, sore boobs, broken sleep (nothing compared to later, but I was not to know that), and a foreboding sense of the unknown. There was incessant preparation, and decisions to make: pregnancy yoga, perineal massage, hypnobirthing, slings, maternity and then nursing clothes, baby things. When I tried to explain to my husband, who continued through life physically unimpaired, I could see that though he tried to understand and sympathise, he didn't quite 'get it'. I realised then that what I was experiencing was perhaps not possible to translate. That this language of biology, of creating, preparing, and planning was something that only *I* was learning in this strange new land called Motherhood.

I so wanted him to understand, to know the visceral moments in my life: the flush of blood as it pulsed through me, the pains in my skin, the deep ache in my groin as the birth grew closer. All the fears, anxieties and niggles. I was crossing a threshold and, although he was right there, I felt so alone.

After our son was born, I went through three months of excruciating breast pain trying to feed an undiagnosed tongue-tied baby. I beat myself up about my 'failed' home birth and the fact that breastfeeding was so hard. I was a 'bad mother' and my body had let me down. In contrast, my husband was besotted and seemed to have fallen seamlessly into parenting.

Everything had changed; where I had once been an autonomous person, I was dependent on him for everything, even the basics, such as taking a pee, eating and going out anywhere *alone*.

In hindsight, our son was actually a relatively easy baby and we managed trips for lunch, visits to museums and even the theatre. But something had changed between us. It didn't seem that my husband understood quite how consumed I felt by motherhood. More than anything, I needed affirmations of what I was, that I was a 'good mother', that I was doing OK, that I was good enough. I deeply wanted to see that look of admiration on his face, the connection, the desire, the wanting me. But though he assured me as much as he could, I still felt entirely displaced by my own feelings of inadequacy.

This aloneness was probably the beginning of the ache that invaded my early months as a mother. I felt I was drowning in milk and nappies; the lack of sleep was so, so hard. And though my husband sat by my side and was as hands-on as he could be, the hard truth was that it seemed as if this was not happening to *us*, but to *me*.

I was doing everything. *I* was managing it all. I was earning the money, trying to write and also to parent with all the skill I could muster. I was trying for the impossible: to keep working, to be the best mother and to use no childcare other than family. Fortunately, the impossible is made possible through impossible thinking. With grandparents' help, we began to weave together a new life, stitching through elements of the old to make it better. Evenings out were a salve to remind us of the connection we once had outside parenting and domesticity.

Our society does little to create viable and sustainable models of family life. There is so much around shared leave, part-time work models and emphasis on family that needs to change. But we should also ask whether we fall into these gendered roles by nature or nurture. How should we decide who does what, and why?

Friends tell me of husbands who suddenly need the toilet when it's time to do chores; who use the TV as a childminder; who feed the kids whatever is easy instead of cooking something nutritious or who expect their wives to supply detailed instructions or dishes whipped up ahead of time. Fathers who never pack the nappy bag, but expect it to be ready and stuffed with everything they need; who assume that social events get updated automatically in the family calendar; who never organise a birthday party, but who are happy to be the 'fun' parent and join in the games.

These are the things – the planning, the worrying, the 'mental load' as some call it – that cannot be left undone. The cascade of obligations seems relentless. But is this about an objective disparity or is it rather a matter of priorities? Am I doing all this because I have to, because no one else will, because I want to, or because I think I can do it better than him?

At home, we argue. About dishes, about laundry, school pick-ups; about who does more. I've kept score. I've been passive aggressive. I've made rotas and to-do lists. I've done everything I can to ensure that I don't get 'taken advantage' of, and that I remain 'autonomous'. Sometimes I can't tell whether I'm fighting for myself, for all women (including my mother and grandmothers) or if I'm just being difficult or ungrateful.

A friend once told me that you couldn't compare apples to oranges. She was a stay-at-home mum; her life was seemingly clear-cut. She had apples and he had oranges. My life seems to be a bit of apple and a bit of orange and a whole lot of pear. How on earth could I stop comparing my life with his, and wanting what he had? Maybe that wasn't the answer at all.

I thought I had made peace with being a mother and all that that entailed. But standing at the sink, some six years into the experience of having children and the veteran of many sleepless nights, I can no longer make out what's fair. I dump the dishes in the dishwasher, even though the clock is ticking and our children need to get to school. I have a point to make and I'm not about to back down. My husband is probably confused by my reaction. He is tired too and perhaps frustrated that I don't care about a clean sink as much as a fully stacked fridge. My belly is full of fire and indignation. I shout at him, storm off, crying.

In the living room, I'm ashamed that I have frightened the children. I listen as my husband calms them down and, despite the anger, I want to feel some of his tenderness too. I am mourning the couple we once were, unsullied by realities of life; an idyllic love. But in the quest for fairness, perhaps it is exactly our different experiences that will allow us to see each other as we really are?

I pick up that chipped mosaic piece from last night, that interrupted moment of intimacy. Touch is the language we speak with our children before they have words. With our partners it is also a language: of love, desire, pleasure, *want*. In parenting, it becomes a place of grounding, reconciliation and reconnection. What one touch can do, a hundred words sometimes cannot. But can we hold the glance long enough, or make that touch deep enough before we are interrupted? It is a process of constant erosion and constant reseeding.

I walk back into the kitchen, and remind myself that maybe I will never quite resolve this question of what is fair or equal – but that love, connection and this life together, gaps and all, is so much more than that. I place a piece back into the mosaic. It is cracked, but its sharp edges catch the light and make it gleam.

SOMETIMES THE OTHER WAY AROUND

Joanne Limburg

What most people know about autism they have learned from stories, many of them stories about mothers.

When autism first came into public consciousness in the 1960s, the stories most commonly told were of bad, unloving mothers, 'refrigerator mothers' who created such a harsh emotional environment that their children shut down inside, dead both to the world and to their own human feelings. As long as they remained in circulation, these stories did great harm. Fortunately, in all but a few countries, they were overwritten by new stories, in which the Bad Mothers were replaced by good, heroic Autism Mothers, battling for their (usually male) children. In some versions of this story, particularly the earlier ones, autism is seen as the antagonist, from which the mother must rescue her child. In others, the mother must battle external forces on behalf of her autistic child.

In recent years, a new subgenre has emerged, in which the mother discovers that she is herself autistic, both an Autism Mother and an Autistic Mother. I know quite a few autistic women who are mothers and, in most cases, that is their story: first the child's diagnosis, then their own. My own story is something different.

Motherhood didn't begin well for me. I went into it knowing that I suffered from depression and anxiety, and aware that I might struggle more than most, but my desire to have a child was greater than any fear I had. A miscarriage exacerbated my anxieties, and by the middle of my second pregnancy, I could barely cross a road, walk down a flight of stairs or swallow a mouthful of food without being assailed by visions of myself getting hit by a car, falling or choking. My GP told me that I had to go back on my antidepressants or risk not being able to look after my baby. I took the medication, and my anxiety reduced a little. I wanted to do everything right. I was the biggest swot in the maternity class. I bought a birthing ball; I slept on my left side to get the baby in the best position; I attended a breastfeeding workshop where we were told that it was by far the best thing for your baby and that we could all do it . . .

This is the set-up to another familiar story, and you know where it's heading – towards an emergency C-section, five days in a transitional care ward and three months of tearful struggle that ended with my son refusing the breast altogether. His father seemed competent at everything – changing him, bottle-feeding him, reading his cries – so if I couldn't nurse him, what use was I? I loved him desperately, but any confidence I had in my ability to look after him was draining away.

Despite the wonderful moments when he slept peacefully on me or smiled at the sight of my face, I felt that he was better off in someone else's hands.

My economic privilege enabled me to pass him to people more expert than me. We had a postnatal doula for the first few weeks and after I was diagnosed with an underactive thyroid five months after the birth, we hired a part-time nanny who stayed with us for a year. It felt like a massive admission of failure.

My son, meanwhile, didn't seem aware that he had a substandard mother. Once I had accepted that I was bottle-feeding, we got on very well. He was not hard to get on with. He smiled early and often, found my attempts at singing or goofing around very entertaining, and – what was most extraordinary to me – seemed to have an instinctive understanding of how to interact with another person. Even before he could talk, he would carry on his side of the conversation by kicking his legs against his chair or his buggy. An exchange would go something like:

Me: Hello!

Him: Smile, kick, kick, kick.

Me: How are you?

Him: Smile, kick, kick, kick.

Me: Shall we go out to the shops now?

Him: Smile, kick, kick, kick, etc., etc.

During our talk–kick conversations, I came to understand something that I had never previously realised, which is that it's the back-and-forth rhythm that makes a conversation a conversation, and not the content, no matter how interesting. I wondered why I hadn't realised this before, when it was so obvious to my preverbal child.

When he was eighteen months old, I got myself a diagnosis – of obsessive-compulsive disorder. It explained my extreme anxiety, my avoidant behaviour and the harsh judgements I made about myself, but it didn't explain why my tiny son seemed to read me so effortlessly, when I had to concentrate to read him. I remember the lunchtime when I realised this. A few spoonfuls in, he made a choking noise; I visibly started and began to panic; he saw my face, stopped making the noise, and grinned. He was only just beginning to form sentences, but he had figured out that I reacted to that particular noise in a dramatic way, and had decided to trigger that reaction. It was a practical joke.

As he got older and more verbal, he would keep returning to my face and the odd things it apparently did. 'Why is your face like that?' he would ask. By the time he was four and a half, this had become 'Why are you worried?' At six, he observed that 'I just saw your face change. You did that thing with your eyes when it looks like you're cross but you're not really cross.' He was right: like a lot of autistic women, I have a bad case of Resting Bitch Face.

When my son was five, my brother took his own life. I was shattered, and left with so many questions about our family, our shared childhood and the diffi-culties we'd both had. My brother had been diagnosed with ADHD as an adult. I wondered if that applied to me too, but it didn't seem to fit. Then I discovered a website about the way Asperger's Syndrome (a form of autism) manifests itself in women, and for the first time, I saw myself. When I was forty-two and my son was nine, I finally got my diagnosis.

My son is sixteen now, and I asked him to help me with this essay (for a fair cut of the fee, of course). I handed him a print-out of a National Autistic Society webpage, called 'Understanding an Autistic Parent: A Guide for Sons and Daughters'. It consisted of answers to commonly asked questions, about parents who don't seem to understand what people mean, or get cross when their child plays loud music, or stressed when they bring friends home. I asked my son to add his comments.

There were very few of them. Next to 'Mum keeps on about school all the time and shouts at me if I don't do things straight away', he wrote, 'Not this.' In the section about loud music, he underlined the words 'sensitive hearing' and wrote, 'Not with anything I do, just loud noises in general' (a sensitivity that, incidentally, he shares). Next to 'My mum doesn't seem to know if I'm feeling a bit down. Why is that?' he put, 'Sometimes the other way around; I say, "No, I'm fine"', which is what he has to do when I can't read his face and worry that I've missed something. His only strong agreement is with the statement 'Mum gets stressed if something unexpected happens', which has been annotated on both sides: in the left margin, with an arrow and 'very this' and in the right margin, with another arrow, 'e.g. delayed trains'. It's true: I don't mind surprises if they're pleasant, but travel disruption freaks me out.

There is, of course, a big question behind all these little ones: how has my autism affected my son? It's hard to know. What I can say is that I always knew I was different, feared that my difference was bad, and was determined to protect my son from it. When he was a baby, I shared his care with other people who I felt could compensate for what I lacked. When he was at school, I did my best to maintain good relationships with other mothers, even when I found this difficult and painful, because I didn't want him to lose out on friendships. As he's grown older, more articulate, and more able to do things for himself, it has become easier. I've come to understand that my anxieties around his well-being come out of traumatic stories that belong to me and my brother, and that I need to hold these separate from the story of my son and his mother.

He's my son, but he's his own person. A non-autistic but nonetheless very logical person, who is taking science A levels. He response to the question of how my autism has affected him was a scientist's answer: cautious, rational and evidence-based. He wrote, 'I've always lived with an autistic mother, so I don't have living with a non-autistic mother to compare.' Another fair point: he has only one mother, and she happens to be autistic. He's not looking for another one though; to my surprise, he accepts me, our relationship, and the ongoing story we're improvising together. The more conventional tale might involve a neurotypical mother and her autistic son. But in some stories, like ours, it's the other way around.

MISFIT

MiMi Aye

I gave them foreign faces, foreign names.

It was me who made them 'Others', not their white, blond father who blends in.

It was me who expelled them into a country that no longer welcomes them.

(But did it ever?)

I was born in the seaside town of Margate; my family moved to the suburbs of Kent a few years afterwards and it's where I've been ever since, apart from three short years at college.

I was five years old the first time I was told to go back to my own country. I'm forty now and I've never forgotten his face and name. Benjamin – scruffy Ben, grubby Ben, perpetually sniffing Ben – who somehow always wore a tracksuit top when the rest of us were in uniform. But his face was white, and his name was white, and so he belonged, whereas I did not.

At that age, I had not yet been outside the UK, but I knew exactly what it meant when he told me to go back to my own country.

My daughter is six years old. Together, we watched *Doctor Who* and she asked me, without pausing, 'Mummy, is the baddie the man with the brown skin or the man with the normal skin?'

White skin is normal, brown skin is not. My daughter is six and already she knows this.

What else is normal? Having sausages and baked beans for tea. My three-year-old son dives in with gusto, grabs a handful of beans and I yell at him, 'For goodness' sake, use your flipping fork!' But my side of the family hails from Burma, where we use our hands to eat almost everything, even noodles. Why am I trying to impose Western conventions on children who are half and half? I feel myself deflate and I mumble, 'It's OK, just make sure you use a fork when you're at school.'

Most mothers say that they don't know what they're doing and they're making it up as they go along, but I have the added thrill of not knowing how to bring up kids in two different languages and two different cultures. I want to, God knows I do. Talking of God, I'm theoretically Buddhist, my husband's an atheist, and others on his side of the family are ostensibly Christian. How and when should we even broach the subject of religion? The six-year-old has RE lessons; she's currently learning about Judaism. She asks us both what we believe in, and I point at the small shrine on the highest shelf in our living room and say, 'That's Lord Buddha – he's here to keep us safe and he looks after everyone.' So far, that's proved good enough for her, but I am uneasy.

She is in Year 2 now: homework to contend with, SATs looming. She sits at the dining table, carefully forming each number. She joins each nought at the bottom, and a dim memory floats into my head: something I once read that said that people who did that had criminal tendencies. I give myself a mental slap.

She asks me to go through each question with her, and writes down each answer, and I find myself twitching whenever she gets anything wrong. I swore I wouldn't be a Tiger Mum, that I'd be cool and laid-back, but sometimes it's all I can do to stop myself from wresting the pencil from her tiny hand and doing it myself. I need to let her know that it's OK to fail and that everyone makes mistakes, but it's so very hard when there's an inherent urge to nag. 'Twice as good to be half as good' is the immigrants' proverb that rings through my head.

My own mum, the actual immigrant, walks into the room and, in Burmese, she asks her granddaughter about her day. My daughter pauses and I think she hasn't understood, but then she replies in English and I'm overwhelmed by a swirl of pride and shame – pleased that she knew exactly what her grandmother had said, but pinned by a two-pronged shame that I had doubted her and that it's not me teaching her my mother('s) tongue.

I bury my shame, as always, and she starts chattering excitedly about her school summer fair. The next week-end we're there, holding dripping ice-cream cones, as the Music Club troupe in front of us performs songs from *The Greatest Showman*. The six-year-old somehow knows all the words, and she lustily sings along. She asks if we can get hold of the film as she's not actually seen it yet, though I have, on a business trip earlier in the year.

My first inclination is to say, 'Yes, of course', but I remember the storyline about an interracial relation-ship, just like Mummy and Daddy's, except forbidden, and riddled with conflict and pain. How old should your child be before you break her heart? Tell her that the love between her parents used to be frowned upon, in some places even illegal? She's only six – is it selfish and wrong of me to want her ignorance to be bliss for just a little while longer? I bite my lip and say, 'No, you're too young, we'll get it another time', and she shrugs in puzzlement and walks off, singing.

That night she asks me about Brexit – she's heard about it at school. The general consensus seems to be that it's a bad thing; she claims she's going to kick Boris Johnson in the bum and she cackles to herself. I smile weakly and think back to the day of the referendum. Heavily pregnant with her little brother, I waddled to the polling station, where most of the other voters gave me dirty looks – one of them literally clutched her pearls. I guess I represented everything they wanted to escape.

Later that day, I had cramps and ended up in hospital, which meant neither my husband nor my mother could vote as they rushed to my side. A false alarm in the end, and I was sent home to rest, but we stayed up most of the night to watch the results roll in, and sensed our futures drift away. I blamed myself for my husband's and mother's lost votes, but it wouldn't have made any difference in the end, and ours was one of the five boroughs in London that voted Leave.

Four days later, I lay on a table, paralysed from the waist down as I was meticulously cut open. I stared at the blooming red stain that was reflected in the shiny ceiling, while white men in white masks with knives casually joked about which way the ballot had gone, and I tried not to cry. I could feel my gorge rising, and I knew it was partly the effect of the anaesthetic, and partly the feeling of despair. Of guilt. Of worry. Of how irresponsible it was that I had brought not one but two children into an increasing shitshow.

Two children who wouldn't fit in, no matter what they did or said, and who would be told, like me, to go back to their own country, a country they had not yet visited.

I gave them foreign faces, foreign names. Unshed tears constantly prick at my eyes.

MATERNAL LANDSCAPES

Carolina Alvarado Molk

I have a picture from the first time I went out alone after my son was born. In it, I'm holding a plastic cup half full of the cheap white wine I sipped cautiously, counting out the minutes before I'd be back home and nursing. I'm wearing red lipstick, but my eyes are tired, and you can tell I'm nervous to be out in the world, suddenly alone, for the first time.

How fortuitous, I thought, that in this reading – my first outing since the baby – the author chose to talk about writing and motherhood. I felt a secret thrill to be sitting there, watching this sophisticated and successful woman saying precisely the things I needed to hear. She talked about how her writing had changed since having children – how in those first years she made do with what was available to her: with music, with something glimpsed through a window, with art pieces in museums she could stroll through with a child.

I felt almost sly, as if I was getting away with something, sitting in that crowd sipping wine as if I were still my old self: not one person in that auditorium knew that under my coat my breasts were swollen with milk and sore, that I was a person untethered, full of love and newly fragmented.

Months later, at a different talk, I listened to an author speak about 'landscapes of feeling'. She handed us poorly Xeroxed maps of extensive fictional worlds as part of the reading. Among the replicas was a hand-drawn map consisting of a single room. Where others signalled mountain ranges, and oceans, and evil or benign kingdoms, this one marked locales such as 'milk donut' and 'frog chair' and 'the mysteriously infinite pile of shoes'. It was the room in which the author had spent her days with an infant daughter. She made it to remind herself, she said, that 'this place mattered too'. She explained that it was layered, like other landscapes, with contradictions and competing vectors, with wonder and claustrophobia. I brought that copy home.

I collect anecdotes of women writers talking, publicly, shamelessly, about their motherhood, in part because they offer the reassurance I need to feel that it can be done and that I can do it too. I collect them because I hear them now – in a way I didn't, or couldn't, before. I collect them because in that first year their words were the only sounds that could abate the solitude, the incredible loneliness, of early motherhood.

I wasn't at all prepared for the loneliness that came after my family and friends left, after my husband returned to work, after my son and I were left to spend our days together, alone. It's hard to convey just how lonely the sleepless nights were – how desperately I wanted to feel that I could still, when I felt nothing like myself, rejoin the world. There isn't much that can prepare you for the transformation of self, the immediate and irreversible shift in identity, that motherhood requires.

There's a silence around those first months that feels impenetrable. I felt isolated from the friends who'd had children before me – if they'd also felt like this, they never told me. I wondered if they'd had this much trouble, if they'd been desperate or sad or bewildered by all of this change in the way that I was, or if I was somehow getting it all wrong. There's so much internalised pressure to be a certain kind of mom – the kind that only ever experiences joy and wonder and love – that admitting to feeling overwhelmed or angry, or even just bored at times, can feel tantamount to failure. It's that societal pressure to be perfect mothers and to hide our shame when we can't live up to that standard that makes us believe we're failing to begin with. People don't tell you that enough: mothers are made to feel shame no matter what they choose to do.

I couldn't remember having read anything that felt quite like that loneliness. Always, I'd relied on books to help me find a place in the world, to make sense of it. I realised how easily the novels I'd so hungrily consumed skimmed right over a pregnancy, if they mentioned one at all. 'Literature has more dogs than babies, and also more abortions,' Rivka Gatchen wrote. It became clear to me just how shallow and romanticised the fictional relationships I'd encountered were – none came close to reflecting the extremes, the blissful highs and the harrowing lows, of my own experience of motherhood.

Novels and memoirs by women writing artfully and with vulnerability about their motherhood weren't hard to find once I learned where to look. They are many, varied and rich – but it often requires searching through reading lists for *mothers* to find them. Rachel Cusk voices the 'gloomy suspicion that a book about motherhood is of no real interest to anyone except other mothers', and it might be that she's right, but it's an assumption that hasn't been fully tested.

It's true that I'd never set out to find memoirs about motherhood before I became a mother, but neither had I stumbled across them. The independent bookshop nearest me – full of women staff and women readers – stocks Anne Lamott's memoir, *Operating Instructions*, downstairs, in the 'Parenting' section, right next to the board books. Readers don't lightly browse the 'Parenting' shelves for a spontaneous purchase in the way they might the new-paperback or memoir or non-fiction displays, any of which would have been a more accurate categorisation for *Operating Instructions*. It doesn't help that books about motherhood are treated, impossibly, as part of a niche market.

There's a prevalent fear that engaging artistically with a domestic realm will be dismissed as a trivial or superficial pursuit – a sense that these subjects don't lend themselves to artistic creation to begin with, that there's no place for them in our literary landscape. Jenny Offil spoke candidly about these concerns – *Dept. of Speculation* is a slim novel that is not explicitly about motherhood, but it offers us a realistically complex version of it. The format of a narrative presented in fragments, such as Gatchen's *Little Labours*, felt tailored to me, to the bits of time that I had for myself, to the breadth of my reduced attention span. Like Offil's narrator, I too feared venturing past a small radius from home with my newborn; like her, I guiltily mourned the loss of my potential selves, the forgone life of the 'art monster'. These books became the close friends that held these secrets and shared them.

Finding resonance in these books helped me feel sane, by which I mean they made me feel understood. I fantasise that I might have been spared some of the loneliness of those early months had I found them sooner. That my friends and I might have had better, more honest conversations about motherhood had we had their words in our vocabularies. These books helped me find a way back – not to who I was, but to my old longing to write and my literary ambition, to a desire that connected the two halves of my world. They helped me see the new features of my motherhood as inextricable from my writing – as complementary elements of one landscape.

You could argue that the literary scene is changing: publications such as *The Paris Review* and *TLS* have noted an outpouring of literary works about motherhood in recent years and have written about them. Elena Ferrante's novels are a phenomenon all their own. There have been more books about motherhood, more panels, more round tables, more women speaking openly about the practicalities of writing and mothering, and about the overlooked hardships and joys. It's hard to explain the giddiness I felt when I reached the last line of Christine Smallwood's meticulous essay on motherhood, 'Never Done': 'My mother babysat while I wrote this article.' I think it was something like vindication – my husband watched our son while I wrote these words.

LIVING WITH CHILDREN

Tiphanie Yanique

My maternal great-grandmother became a single mother when her husband, a captain, drowned at sea. My grandmothers on both sides had husbands whom they left or who left them. My mother was divorced before I turned five. I come from a long line of divorced women. This is despite the fact that the women in my family were and are very religious – Catholic, Muslim, Evangelical. Being divorced was like a death for them. Except in this death you stuck around to feel the pain of it.

Getting divorced from my children's father felt suicidal. What my marriage had done, what it was supposed to do, was make me and my husband one. Divorce meant killing that one – to make two again. I felt pretty dead afterwards. It doesn't help that Google, almost a year later, still lists me as being married. No matter how much I email Google, or get my cousin who works for Google to email his colleagues, Google just keeps showing me as married to that man. Which confirms that I must be dead. Because the internet has no idea that post-divorce Tiphanie exists.

'I hate the idea of being divorced,' I told one aunt.

'Love the idea of being happy,' she said.

'I don't want to be alone,' I told another aunt.

'Don't worry. You're one of us,' she said. She didn't mean because I was surrounded by family, as she clarified: 'If you want another husband, it won't be hard. But do you?'

'Do you want to get married again?' I asked a cousin.

'For what?' she laughed. 'I have my kids.'

Some of the women in my family have been divorced multiple times. Me? I've done it twice. But afterwards, we still have our kids. Because the real point wasn't to be married, it was to be a mother – this is what my women were trying to tell me. Marriage was a convention, one that controlled us women. But motherhood? Well, that was organic, biological. It controlled us only as much as we let it.

And yet, motherhood takes everything from me. But whose fault is that? Mine alone. Because giving to my kids feels like life. Been that way from the start. The first thing I did for my first child when he was born was breastfeed him. I did it immediately. And I did it until I bled. I did it until that boy sucked my nipple to actual rawness and even the La Leche breastfeeding fanatic who came to visit said, 'Well, looks like that baby is trying to kill you.' But I didn't stop. I breastfed him for eighteen months. Breastfed my daughter and younger son the same.

Was I giving my life? Yes. All my divorced foremothers were givers. Helpers. It doesn't take much therapy to see that this might be why at least some of our marriages failed. We gave but often didn't know how to receive, or didn't choose partners who gave to begin with. But we givers were made for motherhood. My breasts were giving trees, just like that psychopath book people keep giving to kids. I never feared that my breasts would get messed up after nursing – this is what my breasts were for. The way they looked after nursing is how they were meant to look. During breastfeeding my then husband would look on with envy – 'They aren't mine any more,' he would say and say, until I finally told him that they never were.

So when, earlier this year, I had my first mammogram ever at forty-one, I went into that breast-imaging centre with cockiness – me and my boobs had done the real work. Not being sexy for husbands; being food for babies. And anyone who ever googled (thanks again, Google!) breastfeeding and breast cancer knew that the former prevented the latter. 'Does breast cancer run in your family?' the nurse asked, the forms asked, the doctor asked. No, it does not. What runs in my family is divorce. But still, the call came. I needed to go back for more imaging. This made no sense to me. Not only had I breastfed three children, I had also recently gone through what my very seasoned divorced divorce lawyers said was one of the worst divorces they'd ever seen. I already didn't exist any more, so I couldn't get a potentially terminal illness. And besides, no way the universe would cancer up a divorced mother of three.

A google search (Google!) showed me that if the doctor had asked for a biopsy that meant they'd found something scary, but they'd only asked for imaging. So off I went. This time a tech came in, a nurse came in, a doctor came in and then another doctor. 'You need a biopsy,' said the last one. He was wearing a wedding ring. And I wanted to beat him to death with the imaging wand. Because how dare he be alive and married when I was divorce-dead and maybe going to be really dead.

I went for the biopsy. It burned. It scraped. The doctor took out parts of me that had never been touched. I might as well have been a cadaver – except that the anaesthetic didn't sink and I was screaming and cursing the doctor's own mother during it all. When I sat in the room trying to remember how to put on my clothes, I realised I had told almost nobody about what was going on with me. I'd been equally private with my divorce. But, as with that divorce, I had now reached a point where I could no longer live as though nothing devastating was going on. So, I told my immediate uppers at work, I told my close friends – that these two groups overlapped was suddenly a life-giving gift.

My friend at work said, 'You have to tell your boyfriend.' Which is when I realised I had a boyfriend. Which is to say, this was when I realised that, despite Google, I wasn't dead. I was alive. And I wanted to stay that way. Not that the universe ever gave a shit about what I wanted. I hadn't wanted to get divorced, but there I was.

'You are one of us,' said my best friend. And by that she didn't mean I was like her, though I am; or that my kids would make me feel whole – though they sometimes do. My bestie clarified: 'If it comes to it, I will come get the kids.' Because she is a mother, so of course she knew what my greatest worry was.

One of my aunts took me home with her after the biopsy. She made sure I slept. I couldn't lift my three-year-old. I couldn't hug the five-year-old or the eight-year-old. 'Be careful of my breast,' I told them. 'I had a procedure.' Really, my body had been theirs until this moment. They could always climb on me. Hang on me. Sleep beside me at night. We bathed together – sometimes all together, in my big tub. The older ones saw me breastfeed the younger. 'This is how I first fed you,' I'd told them. This is what breasts are for. But now the kids touched me gently. Like I was old. Like I was dying. Like I was already dead.

'Will I have breasts?' my daughter asked.

'Yes,' I told her.

'Will I nurse a baby?'

'If you want that to be part of your mothering,' I told her. 'If you want to be a mother,' I remembered to say.

The head nurse called a week later to tell me the results. 'I have good news,' she said.

'I have three kids,' I said back to her, because I wanted her to understand that good news for me really had to be the best kind. 'And I'm a single mother,' I said. 'Divorced.'

'It's benign,' she said.

I started to cry. 'I have been dying,' I said.

'I know,' the nurse said. 'Of course, you were. The mothers, they always are.'

ACKNOWLEDGEMENTS

Books are always the work of many hands, but none more so than this one. Thanks, first and foremost, to the incredible list of authors who agreed to write for us, and then did so with such heart and soul. It's been a privilege to spend time talking about your wonderful writing.

The team at Elliott & Thompson have been an absolute pleasure to work with, and my thanks go to Sarah Rigby and Pippa Crane for their insight and guidance, Melissa Four for the lovely cover design, and Emma Finnigan for getting the word out. Most of all, thank you to Olivia Bays for commissioning this book and then working on it with such fervour, insight and good humour. It seems unfair that it's just my name on the cover.

Thank you to my agent Hayley Steed for not flinching when I decided to throw an extra book into an already busy year. Finally, thanks to the families – made, dreamed-of, chosen, reconstituted, resented, adored – behind these stories.

CONTRIBUTOR BIOGRAPHIES

Katherine May is an author of fiction and memoir whose most recent works have shown a willingness to deal frankly with the more ambiguous aspects of parenting. In *The Electricity of Every Living Thing* she explored the challenges – and joys – of being an autistic mother, and sparked a debate about the right of mothers to ask for solitude. In *Wintering*, she looks at the ways in which parenting can lead to periods of isolation and stress. She lives with her husband and son in Whitstable, Kent.

Michelle Adams grew up in the United Kingdom, but is currently based in Limassol, Cyprus, where she lives with her family and two cats. She has written two psychological thrillers, and her next release, *Little Wishes*, is a love story set in Cornwall, stretching across five decades of life. Michelle writes full-time, and can occasionally be found working as a scientist.

Javaria Akbar is a freelance writer. She has contributed to the *Guardian*, the *Telegraph*, BuzzFeed, Refinery29, The Pool, Munchies, Vice, Dazed Beauty and more. She is also a part-time cookery writer and mother of two.

Charlene Allcott is a graduate of the Penguin Random House WriteNow programme and author of two novels: *The Single Mum's Wish List* and *More Than a Mum*. She was born in Croydon and now lives in Brighton.

British-born to Burmese parents, **MiMi Aye** has always moved between two worlds, and her life at home in the suburbs of London with her husband and two children is very different from the life spent with her family back in Burma. Her latest book, *Mandalay: Recipes and Tales from a Burmese Kitchen*, was chosen by the *Observer*, the *Financial Times*, and the *Mail on Sunday* as one of their Best Books of 2019, and was described by Nigella Lawson as 'a really loving and hungry-making introduction to a fascinating cuisine' and by Tom Parker-Bowles as 'a glorious revelation . . . autobiography, history and recipes all rolled into one magnificent whole . . . a brilliant, beguiling book'. She is on Twitter and Instagram as @meemalee and on Facebook at www.facebook.com/itsmeemalee.

Jodi Bartle is a New Zealander who has lived in London for nearly twenty years. In-between, she has written for Vice, i-D, Chanel, Quintessentially, Gaggenau, Selfridges, Sunseeker and The London Mother on photography, interior design, fashion, art, travel and babies, in both print and online form. She is currently part of the journalistic and editorial team at MCCA's Diversity & the Bar, a US-based publication that highlights diversity issues in the legal profession, and spills all her embarrassing parenting stories via her blog theharridan.

Playwright, screenwriter and prose writer **Sharmila Chauhan**'s work is often a transgressive meditation on love, sex and power. Her plays include *Be Better in Bed*, *The Husbands* (Soho Theatre), *Born Again/Purnajanam* (Southwark) and *10 Women* (Avignon Festival). Both her short films (*Girl Like You*, *Oysters*) were produced by Film London and her feature *Mother Land* was long-listed for the Sundance Writers' Lab. Sharmila also has a degree in pharmacy and a PhD in clinical pharmacology. She lives in London with her husband, son and daughter and cat Tashi. You can find her at www.sharmilathewriter.com

Josie George lives with her son in a tiny terraced house in the urban West Midlands. Her days are watchful, restricted and often solitary, in a large part because of the debilitating disability she's had since she was a child, but also because she's discovered that a slow, quiet life has much to teach her. Josie's brave and singular memoir will be published by Bloomsbury in early 2021. In the meantime, she is working on a novel and writes blogs about her powerful and gently subversive way of looking at the world at bimblings.co.uk. You can find her on Twitter as @porridgebrain.

Leah Hazard is a serving NHS midwife, author of the *Sunday Times* bestselling memoir *Hard Pushed: A Midwife's Story*, and mother of two children. She lives in Scotland with her family and continues to write about the many wonders and challenges of women's journeys to motherhood.

Joanne Limburg has published non-fiction, poetry and fiction. Her most recent books are the memoir *Small Pieces: A Book of Lamentations* (Atlantic Books) and the poetry collection *The Autistic Alice* (Bloodaxe Books). She lives in Cambridge with her husband and now-teenage son.

Susana Moreira Marques is a writer and an award-winning journalist. Her work has appeared in the *Guardian*, *BBC World Service*, *Granta*, *Tin House*, *Lettre International* and many other publications. Her non-fiction book, *Now and at the Hour of our Death*, was praised as a genre-busting debut and was translated into English, French and Spanish. Her new book, about motherhood, is coming out in Portuguese in May 2020. She lives in Lisbon with her partner, two daughters and one stepson.

Dani McClain reports on race and reproductive health. She is a contributing writer at *The Nation* and a fellow with Type Media Center (formerly the Nation Institute). Her writing has appeared in outlets including *The Atlantic*, *Time*, *Slate*, *Colorlines*, EBONY. com, and The Rumpus. In 2018, she received a James Aronson Award for Social Justice Journalism. Her work has been recognized by the National Lesbian and Gay Journalists Association, the National Association of Black Journalists, and Planned Parenthood Federation of America. She was a staff reporter at the *Milwaukee Journal Sentinel* and has worked as a strategist with organizations including Color of Change and Drug Policy Alliance. Her book, *We Live for the We: The Political Power of Black Motherhood*, was published in 2019 by Bold Type Books (formerly Nation Books).

Hollie McNish is a writer based between Cambridge and Glasgow. She has published three poetry collections, *Papers*, *Cherry Pie* and *Plum*, and one poetic memoir on politics and parenthood, *Nobody Told Me*, about which *The Scotsman* said: 'The world needs this book'. Her next book, *Slug: And Other Things I've Been Told To Hate*, will be published in February 2021 and is a collection of poems, memoir and short stories. She normally likes her tea with two sugars.

Saima Mir is an award-winning writer and journalist. A recipient of the Commonwealth Broadcast Association's World View Award, Saima has worked for the BBC, and has written for numerous publications including the *Guardian*, *The Times* and the *Independent*. Her essay

'A Woman of Substance' appeared in Picador's *It's Not About The Burqa*. Her first novel, *The Khan*, is due to be published by Point Blank and has been optioned by the BBC.

Carolina Alvarado Molk was born in the Dominican Republic, and raised in Brooklyn, NY. She holds a PhD in English from Princeton University, and is currently working on a collection of essays about her experiences growing up undocumented.

Emily Morris is an author and freelance journalist from Manchester, UK. *My Shitty Twenties*, her memoir of single parenthood, was named a *Guardian* readers' favourite book of 2017, and has been optioned for a TV series, which is in development. She is currently working on a novel.

Jenny Parrott is publishing director of Point Blank, the literary crime imprint at prize-winning independent publisher Oneworld, and she teaches creative writing. She also writes Second World War-set sagas under the names Kitty Danton and Katie King, with series currently at Orion and HarperCollins.

Huma Qureshi is an award-winning author, journalist and blogger. Her journalism has appeared in the *Guardian* and the *Observer*, as well as several other national publications including *The Times*, the *Independent* and *New Statesman*. Her first book, *In Spite of Oceans*, a collection of short stories, won The John C Laurence Award from The Authors' Foundation. Her blog, Our Story Time, is a collection of her personal writing.

Peggy Riley is a playwright and writer. Her novel, *Amity & Sorrow*, is about how we make families, however strange they might appear. Her short fiction has been shortlisted for prizes including Bridport and the Costa Short Story prize. Her work for theatre has been produced off-West End and on the fringe, on tour and in community, for radio and site-specifically. Originally from Los Angeles, Peggy lives on the North Kent coast with a husband and an enormous golden retriever. You can find her at www.peggyriley.com.

Michelle Tea is the author of over a dozen books in multiple genres. Her essay collection *Against Memoir* won the PEN/America Dimonstein-Spielvogel Award for the Art of the Essay. Her most recent title is the children's book *Tabitha and Magoo Dress Up Too*, inspired by the international Drag Queen Story Hour phenomenon, which she created. She is the creator of multiple literary projects, including the ongoing Sister Spit tours, the online parenting zine Mutha, and the Amethyst Editions imprint at The Feminist Press.

Tiphanie Yanique is the author of the poetry collection *Wife*, which won the 2016 Bocas Prize in Caribbean poetry and the United Kingdom's 2016 Forward/Felix Dennis Prize for a First Collection. Tiphanie is also the author of the novel *Land of Love and Drowning*, which won the 2014 Flaherty-Dunnan First Novel Award from the Center for Fiction, the Phillis Wheatley Award for Pan-African Literature, and the American Academy of Arts and Letters Rosenthal Family Foundation Award, and was listed by NPR as one of the Best Books of 2014. *Land of Love and Drowning* was also a finalist for the Orion Award in Environmental Literature and the Hurston-Wright Legacy Award. She is also the author of a collection of stories, *How to Escape from a Leper Colony*, which won her a listing as one of the National Book Foundation's 5Under35. Her writing has also won the Bocas Award for Caribbean Fiction, the Boston Review Prize in Fiction, a Rona Jaffe Foundation Writers Award, a Pushcart Prize, a Fulbright Scholarship and an Academy of American Poet's Prize. She has been listed by the Boston Globe as one of the sixteen cultural figures to watch out for and her writing has been published in the *New York Times*, *Best African American Fiction*, *The Wall Street Journal*, *American Short Fiction* and other places. Tiphanie is from the Virgin Islands and an associate professor at Emory University.